Ken Weber

RUNNING PRESS
PHILADELPHIA • LONDON

Printed in Canada

9 8 7 6 5 4 3 2 1
Digit on the right indicates the number of this printing

Library of Congress Control Number: 2005910397

ISBN-13: 978-0-7624-2681-2
ISBN-10: 0-7624-2681-0

Cover & Interior design by Joshua McDonnell
Cover & Interior illustrations by Robert L. Price
Typography: Helvetica and Coronet

This book may be ordered by mail from the publisher.
Please include $2.50 for postage and handling.
But try your bookstore first!

Running Press Book Publishers
125 South Twenty-Second Street
Philadelphia, Pennsylvania 19103-4399

Visit us on the web!
www.runningpress.com

Table of Contents

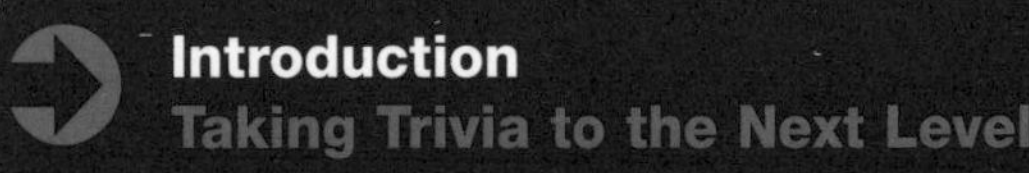

Introduction
Taking Trivia to the Next Level

If you know your trivia, then you know that Mrs. O'Leary's cow was blamed for starting the great Chicago Fire by kicking over a lantern. Ever wondered what happened to the cow? Those swallows that come back to Capistrano every year in March . . . *where have they been, anyway?* Then there's the summer of '61, when the Yankees' Roger Maris kept the whole of America on edge until he finally broke Babe Ruth's home run record. *But whose record did Ruth break?*

That is how *One-up Trivia* works. We start with a classic bit that everybody knows and then move the goalposts by posing the *next* question, the one nobody ever thinks to ask. If someone wants to know, for example, who was first to fly an airplane, for sure you'll reply "The Wright brothers, Wilbur and Orville." But everybody knows that, so *One-up Trivia* asks: "Which one flew the plane?" Or try this One-Up: Hollywood has made more movies about boxing than about any other sport. *What sport comes in second?* Now move to geography: You know that Iran used to be called Persia. *What was it called before it became Persia?*

Of course *One-up Trivia* also gives you the answers. And more. The Wright brothers flew four times that day in Kitty Hawk, and likely would have gone up a fifth or even a sixth time, too, but on the day of that famous first flight they also scored the world's first airplane disaster when the wind tipped *Flyer* over on its back.

That's another thing *One-up Trivia* does: along with the answers to those *next* questions, there are more one-up trivia facts. For example, in our piece on the classic movie/musical *Gentlemen Prefer Blondes* (our one-up question is "Do they really?") we also offer essential information like the fact that blondes actually have more hair strands per square inch than redheads, or any other color for that matter. And when the book explains where the Capistrano swallows come from, there's a lot more fun stuff about things that descend from the air.

One-up Trivia is all about having fun with trivia by coming at it from a completely different angle. So challenge yourself, or better still, use this book to one-up your favorite trivia buff.

By the way, there are some one-ups that still bug us because we can't find the answer. If you happen to know who painted the *floor* of the Sistine Chapel while Michaelangelo was painting the ceiling, please let us know.

Ken Weber

CATEGORY

1

Classic Movies

TITLE
DIRECTOR
CAMERA
DATE
SCENE
TAKE

1

Movie buffs, Hollywood insiders, and historians of the cinema all agree that the first no-holding-back French kiss in a Hollywood movie was delivered unto Natalie Wood by Warren Beatty in *Splendour in the Grass* in 1961.

Who was on the receiving end of the *first* ever movie kiss?

Are There Rules for Kissing?

In 1652, England's Puritan dictator, Oliver Cromwell, made kissing illegal on Sundays. Around 1300, Pope Clement V declared a kiss a mortal sin if it was a step on the way to further activity. (A later Clement—XIV—is noteworthy for deleting toe-kissing from papal ritual.) In the 1930s, the state of Pennsylvania banned movies that showed couples kissing while in a horizontal position. Vertical was okay.

Kissing: The Next Generation?

By 1926, the movie world had obviously overcome any inhibitions: in *Don Juan* that year, John Barrymore besmooched Mary Astor and Estelle Taylor a total of 127 times. In a one-hour reel that averages out to a kiss every 28.4 seconds, which is why there wasn't much of a plot. On the other hand, the plot was prominent in *The Thomas Crown Affair* (1968), and Faye Dunaway and Steve McQueen were still able to get in Hollywood's longest on-screen kiss so far (55 seconds). In India, Bollywood fans had to wait until 1978 to see their first hot screen clutch. That was in *Love Sublime* and it was so controversial the Indian government was dragged into the fuss. Midway through the opening decade of the twenty-first century there were still two major film-producing countries that banned kissing in movies: Iran and Turkey.

Mae Irwin. The popular vaudeville comedienne was smacked on the lips in Thomas Edison's studio in 1896 by actor John Rice in a one-reeler called *The Kiss*. (They didn't bother with focus groups to come up with titles then.) The movie was actually a scene from a stage play, *The Widow Jones*, and got far more press than the play ever did. One reviewer labeled the film "absolutely disgusting" and that was enough to bring people out in droves to see it.

2

Three dogs have their own stars on Hollywood's Walk of Fame. Lassie and Rin Tin Tin come to mind immediately.

Who is the third one?

Did They Live Happily Ever After?

Although both Strongheart and Rin Tin Tin died relatively young, Lassie lived to age 19. Another long-lived animal star is Daisy, the pig seen in the Hobbits' birthday party for Bilbo Baggins in the first *Lord of the Rings* movie (2001), *The Fellowship of the Ring*. Daisy was actually headed for the slaughterhouse when she lucked out and got picked for the scene. On the set, she endeared herself to the crew so strongly that instead of being returned to meet her fate, she was retired to a New Zealand farm to live out her life naturally. (At publication of this book she was still enjoying herself.)

Not Always What They Seem?

Like other Hollywood stars, these dogs had shortcomings known only to the studios. Strongheart had an aversion to howling and a substitute was needed to do voiceovers. Lassie, always so clever that he seemed human, was actually performing for biscuits his trainer had concealed on the human actors. Rin Tin Tin never did get over being shell shocked from the war, and was terrified of guns. His successor, Rin Tin Tin Junior, was terminally lazy. In *The Canine Detective* (1936) Junior captured a gang of bandits unaided but when real robbers broke into the residence of his master and cleaned it out, Rinty Junior slept through the whole thing.

Strongheart. A German shepherd like Rin Tin Tin, but unlike Rinty, who was found whimpering in a World War I trench and brought to America, Strongheart was headhunted. Strongheart, Rin Tin Tin and Lassie (who was male) all got megastar treatment. Rin Tin Tin, for example, was the only dog in America with his own limousine and chauffeur. Of the three, only Strongheart was a bit scary. Not surprising because prior to being "discovered" he'd been trained as an attack dog.

3

Elvis Presley fans were shocked when they first saw him in *Love Me Tender* (1956). The King in overalls behind a plow was not what they were used to from the guy who'd fired them up with hits like "Hound Dog" and "Jailhouse Rock." But the movie's signature tune made them forget all that. "Love Me Tender," a straight lift of a song written about a hundred years earlier, became one of his biggest hits.

What song was "lifted" for the movie?

How Tender does Love Get?

Anyone disinclined to accept the reality of projectile-borne sperm might consider the mating practices of the *Drosophila bifurca*, the giant fruit fly. The male of this species delivers pellets of sperm through the air by means of—for lack of a more scientific term—"the peashooter effect." (Biologists have yet to confirm that the effect is enhanced by a soft rendering of "Love Me Tender.")

Love in All the Wrong Places?

No one will ever know if Legrand G. Capers, M.D., a Civil War surgeon from Mississippi, was anticipating these future lyrics from his state's most famous son, but in an 1874 issue of *The American Medical Weekly*, he reported a situation that, if not tender and sweet, is certainly interesting. In the journal, Dr. Capers described his treatment of a Confederate soldier with a most unfortunate wound: during the Battle of Raymond, in May, 1863, a minié ball had passed through his reproductive organs. A gruesome prospect but hardly worth a journal article were it not for the miniè ball's apparent trajectory. Following its first adventure with the soldier the same bullet penetrated a young lady who had been standing nearby. Weeks later she found herself pregnant and, understandably bewildered, presented herself to Dr. Capers who put two and two together, so to speak. The sperm-carrying miniè was later presented to the Old Courthouse Museum in Vicksburg to be displayed with an insistent testimonial by the good doctor that the phenomenon actually did occur.

"Aura Lee," a ballad from 1861, with lyrics by W.W. Fosdick and music by G.R. Foulton. Often wrongly attributed to Stephen Foster of "My Old Kentucky Home" fame, this soft and gentle love song begins "As the blackbird in the spring." The Presley revision starts, "Love me tender; love me sweet."

4

By September 30, 1955, James Dean had finished his last scenes for *Giant* (1956) and took his brand new Porsche Spyder 550 for a spin on California's Route 466. Dean was not just an American teen idol and a much-adored rebel without a cause, he was a fine actor with—according to *Time* magazine—a "streak of genius." *Giant* would earn him an Oscar nomination as Best Actor, but he would never know that. At 5.59 p.m. that day, he was killed when the Porsche piled into a five-year-old Ford Tudor at high speed. To movie buffs, it was the saddest and most famous car accident of the twentieth century.

Who was driving the Ford?

A *Really* Jinxed Car?

Dean's Porsche ranks high on the spooky scale, but comes in way below the vehicle in which Archduke Ferdinand was assassinated in Serbia in 1914, triggering World War I. Before it was finally scrapped this topless phaeton racked up 13 more deaths and 20 serious injuries.

And all before Stephen King wrote *Christine*.

A Jinxed Car?

Dean's friends had talked of the Porsche giving them a bad feeling well before the accident and before the strange things that followed. When the wreck was stripped for parts, the engine went to a professional racer, Troy McHenry. He totaled in his next event. Another racer, William Eschrid, bought the drive train. Next event—same thing. A third collector bought the front tires. Both blew out on the same trip. California Highway Patrol bought the shell to use as a drive-safely-or-else exhibit for teenagers. It fell off its pedestal and injured a Sacramento high school student.

Dean's unfortunate car crash may be pop culture's best known, but there are other contenders. An embarrassing "first" was earned by none other than Karl Benz while showing off his new invention at an exhibition in Munich in 1885. The internal combustion engine ran well, but he drove the vehicle into a wall. Ten years later, at a horseless carriage demonstration in England, the Anglo-French Motor Car Company won the dubious distinction of causing the world's first auto death by driving over spectator Bridget Driscoll. Three years after that Henry Bliss, the first American victim, stepped off a streetcar near Central Park into the path of an electric-powered taxi.

Donald Turnupseed, a college student on his way home for a visit with family. He survived the crash. The Ford was repairable, but according to police, Dean's Porsche was "crumpled up like an empty cigarette pack." No charges were laid.

5

It's a given among trivia buffs that classic movies produce classic goofs. In *Bullitt* (1968), for example, there is a car chase that set the industry standard with the bad guys in a Dodge Charger being pursued by a Ford Mustang. The Charger loses three wheel covers during the chase and three more when it crashes! Then there's Tom Hanks at Jenny's grave in *Forrest Gump* (1996). "You died on a Saturday morning," says Hanks ("Gump"). But the date on the grave marker fell on a Monday. Even the Oscars are not immune. If it had been left to the engravers of the statuettes, the Oscar for Best Actor at the 1938 awards would have gone to comic book hero Dick Tracy

Whose name was supposed to be on that Oscar?

Or Are Goofs Time-Honored Tradition?

Goofing didn't start with movies. Renaissance painter Jacobo Tintoretto (1518-94) in his "Israelites Gathering Manna in the Desert," has Moses surrounded by fellow Exodus travelers with shotguns slung over their shoulders. However, Tintoretto's "Circumcision," in the Church of Santa Maria del Carmine in Venice, depicts the necessary surgical tools with accuracy, so he batted at least .500.

Doesn't anybody check first?

Could it be that mistakes occur because movie people don't go to history class? The movie *Ray* (2004), so full of scenes from early twentieth century America, is rife with slipups. Like the scene in Georgia, set in 1961, where a policeman drives a Harley-Davidson model that wasn't made until 1984. Or the Ray-Bans on Quincy Jones at the Newport Jazz Festival in 1965—they first appeared in 1990. Then there's the train with double-decker containers that runs in the background when Ray Charles is still a little boy in the 1930s.

Or could it be a simple case of no one noticing until it is too late, as in the great classics, *The Maltese Falcon* (1941) and *The Godfather* (1972). In the former, Peter Lorre's tie changes inexplicably from polka dots to stripes in the same scene, while in the latter, Al Pacino shoots a police chief in the neck, but if you look carefully next time you rent the video, you'll see the bullet hole is in his forehead! The goofiest one of all may be the cast on Jimmy Stewart's leg in *Rear Window* (1954). In one scene it has switched legs!

Spencer Tracy, for his role in *Captains Courageous*. A minor goof really, compared to blunders in movies like the blind man wearing a watch in *The Ten Commandments* (1956) or the factory label on Christ's robe in *The Last Temptation of Christ* (1988).

6

For almost a century now, Hollywood has put out an average of ten films a year in which sports are a major player. Even without Rocky Balboa or *Million Dollar Baby* or *Cinderella Man* or . . . well, you name them . . . it's not hard to figure out that more movies have been made about boxing than any other sport.

What sport comes in second?

Does Wrestling Have an Edge Too?

Just down the coast in Providence RI in the 1930s, in a straight wrestling match—most wrestlers were in it for real then—Stanley Pinto was stretching on the ropes. Just as the bell rang, Pinto got himself all tangled up and succeeded in pinning himself on the mat with shoulders down. The referee counted one-two-three; his opponent, George Zaryoff laughed and said thank you; Pinto lost the appeal. Events like this may explain why wrestling is in the eighth spot on the movie list.

Why Does Boxing Have an Edge?

Studios like boxing because audiences focus better on individuals. Boxing also has many larger than life characters and a run of great stories all the way from the heroic to the improbable—such as the shortest bout on record: a knockout at 10.5 seconds of the first round. That was in Lewiston, Maine, in 1946. Welterweight Al Couture, a notoriously aggressive starter, sprang across the ring at the opening bell and threw a knockout punch while his opponent Ralph Walton, equally notorious for being slow, was still putting in his mouth guard.

Horse racing, well ahead of baseball, which is a logical guess.

Baseball is actually in fifth place behind football and auto racing. Basketball ranks seventh, and golf ninth. Tennis comes in a low eighteenth, but that's still ahead of kickboxing, which is in twenty-ninth spot, tied with fishing. Only one film has ever been made about lawn bowling, an Australian epic in 1992 entitled *Greenskeeping*.

7

L. Frank Baum published *Mother Goose in Prose* way back in 1897, and was somewhat surprised to find he had a hit on his hands. Three years later he made an even bigger splash with a story about a Kansas farm girl who was caught in a tornado and taken away to Munchkinland where she encounters various witches, a tin man, a cowardly lion and other strange characters. The most famous movie version of this book has been in continuous release since 1939.

What is the title of Baum's book?

Ducking the Censors?

Wizard was as pure as *Gone with the Wind* was controversial. *GWTW*, released in 1939, offered what was widely believed to be Hollywood's first ever on-screen "damn," uttered by Clark Gable ("Rhett Butler"). In fact, *Blessed Event* had a character say, "I'll be damned!" in 1932. In 1935, actor Fred Stone, said "Damn you!" in *Alice Adams*, and "damn" was uttered twice in *Pygmalion* in 1938.

Why Is *Oz* Such a Trivia Favorite?

The Wizard of Oz (i.e., the movie) has wonderful tales to tell. MGM wanted Jerome Kern to write the music but he was ill, so Harold Arlen and "Yip" Harburg became the composers. The signature song, "Over the Rainbow", was ordered cut by the enormously opinionated Louis B. Mayer of MGM, but then restored. It won the Oscar for Best Song, but the movie itself lost Best Picture to *Gone with the Wind*. Judy Garland was a fallback choice for the role of Dorothy because MGM wanted Shirley Temple so badly it offered both Clark Gable and Jean Harlow for her in a trade, but Harlow's untimely death put an end to negotiations. Although *Wizard* opened to wide acclaim—on the day of the premiere in New York, there were 15,000 people lined up by 5:30 a.m.—it was a financial flop initially. MGM had bought the rights for a mere $75,000 and production costs were within reason, but it took over 20 years to earn back the investment.

The Wonderful Wizard of Oz. Baum's title is almost never cited accurately, probably because the ""wonderful"" was deleted for the movie. Names from the book get short shrift in the movie too, like Dorothy's surname (Gayle) and the wizard's full name: Oscar Zoraster Phadrig Isaac Norman Henkle Emanuel Ambroise Diggs.

8

Hum the music to “Shall We Dance” from *The King and I* (1956) and fans of classic movies can actually see Deborah Kerr and Yul Brynner swirling about in their minds. Those same fans will tell you the movie is about an American governess hired to look after the royal children of Siam, and in the process warms the heart of their stern father. The governess was Anna Leonowens.

Who was the king?

Where Is Siam?

Siam became Thailand in 1934 (the same year that cortisone was first used to treat arthritis). *The King and I* and a 1999 flick starring Jodie Foster, called *Anna and the King*, are both banned in Thailand.

Anna's Real Job: Was it Birth Control?

Anna was not a governess; she was hired to teach English, and the idea that Mongkut fell for her is pure Hollywood. Had she really had influence in her brief tenure there (1862-68), Anna might have introduced the 600 members of the royal harem to a Victorian fashion that was proving to be an effective, if unintentional, method of birth control: the corset. The invention of metal eyelets had led to extremely tight girdles becoming de rigeur for Victorian ladies. Fashion dictated that waistlines be about 60% of normal so a woman with, say, a 25-inch middle would try to squish down to a svelte 15. The result was contraception by corset. Women moaned to their diaries about arthritis, backaches, constipation, and severe discomfort during performance of "the family duty." According to medical historians, the fashion affected ovulation, for the birth rate among fashionable Victorian women dropped 11% in the 1850s and 26% by 1890. Photos of Anna and several of Mongkut's favorite wives suggest that while she wore a corset, the locals did not. The odds of producing 82 kids in 16 years therefore, seems more than an even possibility, with or without intervention from Anna Leonowens.

Mongkut. (Samdetch Phra Maha Mongkut, in case you need the whole thing.)

When he became king, Mongkut already had 12 children, a low number for royalty of the day, but he had taken a vow of celibacy so that may have held back production. After assuming the throne, Mongkut fathered 82 more in 16 years, an accomplishment that perhaps explains why "Getting to Know You" became a signature song in the movie.

Not a classic movie, but a jazz classic captured on film: The "First Lady of Song," Ella Fitzgerald, was performing live in Berlin when she forgot the lyrics to "Mack the Knife." Her improvisation won her a Grammy (for "Ella in Berlin").

Who wrote those lyrics that Ella forgot?

Think your iPod is compact?

In 1923, HMV in Britain produced playable records small enough to fit inside a toilet paper roll. They were made for Queen Mary's doll house (on view in Windsor Castle). HMV made 92,000 of these tiny records, 35,000 of which were pressings of "God Save the King." That seems an extraordinarily high number of one tune, but then Queen Mary was quite deaf.

Who Needs MP3s?

In a business called the "recording-industry," it's rather interesting that for truly industrial-level production, the Guinness title goes to an Indian singer whose career ended back when 8-track audiotapes were still popular. Between 1948 and 1974, Lata Mangeshker, the hottest female singer in her native country, laid down over 25,000 tracks in twenty different Indian languages and dialects. Yet as fly-right-off-the-shelf sellers, Ms. Mangeshker's recordings take a back seat to the Beatles, whose eponymous 1968 double LP sold two million copies in the first week of release. But even that figure is well back of *John Fitzgerald Kennedy: A Memorial Album.* In December 1963, this vinyl record sold four million copies in five days (at 99 cents). Given the technology of the day, the producers must have begun production well before the late president was assassinated, right?

Berthold Brecht wrote the original lyrics in German for Kurt Weill's *Three-Penny Opera* but American Marc Blitzstein adapted them for the English version, which Ella forgot—and which both Bobby Darin and Louis Armstrong made famous. "Mack the Knife" is a very well known song, and continues to be "covered" by musicians everywhere, but it's nowhere near the position held by the Beatles' "Yesterday." Within twelve years of its release in 1965, "Yesterday" was re-recorded by over 1200 artists and continued to hold the record for "covers" well into the twenty-first century.

CATEGORY

2

Geography

Australia is the world's largest exporter of wool. That's only logical, because Australia has the world's second largest number of sheep.

What country has the largest number of sheep?

Presidential Sheep?

The White House lawn supported a flock of sheep in 1917. Woodrow Wilson thought it a great PR move in the war effort. The sheep produced wool for the Red Cross, and they kept the grass short, thereby releasing gardeners for military service. As with the Australian fence, results were just so-so. The sheep kept the lawn mowed all right, but their very active digestive systems, in addition to fouling the summer breezes, made strolling around the lawns such a challenge that the former gardeners had to be replaced by workers with stoop-and-scoop skills.

During the Eisenhower administration—after the sheep were long gone and the gardeners were back—caretaking staff actively considered a Great Wall or Aussie-type fence for the White House lawn because hordes of squirrels constantly interfered with Ike's daily putting practice.

China, and they beat Australia in the total pig and goat count, too.

Not that Australians are bothered about this, because they have the world's longest fence. It's 3,307 miles long and that's one third longer than China's Great Wall. On the other hand, the Australian barrier was built to keep out wildlife and is performing poorly, while the Great Wall was built to keep out invading Mongols and there hasn't been a Mongol invasion for centuries.

2

Everybody knows this 1881 gunfight in Tombstone, Arizona: On one side were the Earp brothers—Wyatt, Morgan and Virgil—backed up by an on-again-off-again dentist, "Doc" Halliday. Lined up against them were the Clanton brothers, Ike and Billy, and their neighbors, Tom and Frank McLaury.

Where did this legendary gunfight take place?

Where does the phrase "O.K." come from?

Take your pick. One favorite theory is that semi-literate President Andrew Jackson approved documents with "Oll Korrect." Another traces O.K. to President Van Buren's election campaign (he was from Old Kinderhook, NY). Some claim a Choctaw Indian source, and devotees of black history trace it to African languages. Then there's Obadiah Kelly, a railroad freight agent who allegedly got the whole thing started by putting his initials on bills of lading. Possibly more interesting is the sign language used to say O.K. Most Europeans raise a thumb, while most North Americans circle the thumb and forefinger. The difference—for tourists—can be significant. In southern Europe especially, the circled thumb and finger is a sign for a certain exit point in the human anatomy.

Not at the O.K. Corral. That bit of myth was not spun until several years after Wyatt Earp passed away in 1929 (he died in bed). The gunfight actually took place in a vacant lot between Camillus Fly's Rooming House and a private residence. There really was an O.K. Corral in Tombstone but it was down the street. Wyatts worshipful biographer, Stuart Lake, moved the gunfight to the corral, and the city, sensing a tourism opportunity, enlarged the corral site to take in the lot where the gunfight happened.

3

Throughout the Civil War, "Dixie" was sung by soldiers on both sides, although it was—and still is—widely believed to be the official anthem of the Confederacy.

What was the official anthem of the Confederacy?

Anthem Headaches at the Olympics?

Officials in charge of the medal ceremonies at the Olympics love Japan's anthem; it's only 11 bars long. They like Iceland's, too. It's 22 bars long with lyrics by Sveinbjorn Sveinbjornsson (who, fortunately, did not include his name). Ecuador's anthem however, gives the officials shivers because it's a whole 135 bars. A red-hot squad from there could conceivably extend the Olympic medal ceremonies for hours.

"God Save the South," but it never caught on like "Dixie," the real title of which, incidentally, is "I Wish I Was in Dixie's Land." Like "La Marseillaise," a marching song popular in the French Revolution, Dixie was never intended to be an anthem, but also like "La Marseillaise" it was very successful at cranking up passions and thus became an anthem almost by default.

"God Save the Queen," Britain's anthem, is one of the world's best known tunes, probably because the same melody is used for patriotic songs in Germany, Russia, Sweden, Lichtenstein, and the U.S.A. "God Save the Queen" is written in waltz time, but does not seem to make listeners sway back and forth like another waltz-time anthem, "The Star Spangled Banner." But then the music for the U.S. anthem was originally a drinking song, "Anachreon in Heaven," so that may account for the swaying—that, or the mangling the beleagured "Star Spangled Banner" gets from pop singers at sporting events.

4

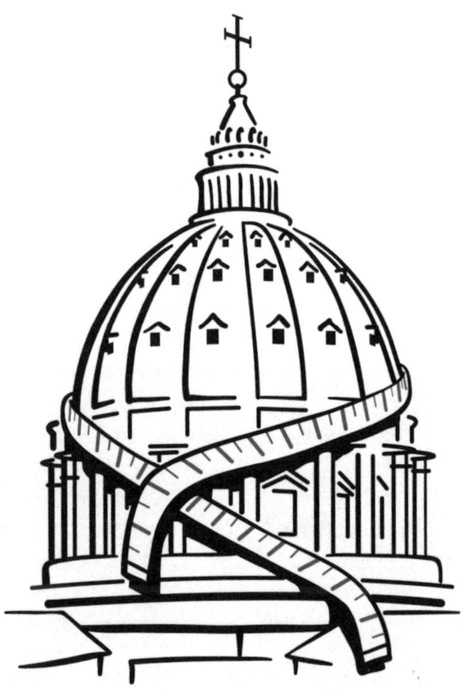

Ask anyone to name the world's largest basilica, and they'll tell you St. Peter's in Rome. It's a slam dunk, really: the floor area of St. Peter's covers about five and a half acres.

No, really, what is the world's largest basilica?

What Is the Largest Synagogue?

The world's largest synagogue is New York's Temple Emanu-El; the largest mosque is Shah Faisal Mosque in Islamabad. Waterton did not climb either of these. He died peacefully in his bed long before they were built.

Scientist or nutcase?

Waterton was a self-taught biologist who is credited with techniques in taxidermy still used today. In the early 1800s, Charles Waterton made three extended trips up the Amazon to capture jungle animals alive in order to study them, but his trapping techniques were unorthodox to say the least. Rather than use a net or noose to catch giant anacondas, for example, he would crawl into their dens and when they attacked, stun them with a fist to the head. He also discovered—by trial and error—that one man alone can hold a 14-foot alligator's jaws shut while sitting on its head.

Our Lady of Peace in Côte d'Ivoire
(formerly the Ivory Coast).

It's in the capital city of Yamoussoukro and beats St. Peter's by almost two acres! St. Peter's, however, is the only basilica in the world known to have experienced an unauthorized climb on the outside by a tourist. In the winter of 1817, Englishman Charles Waterton, shinnied up the dome and hung his mittens on the cross. Pope Pius VII was not amused, even less so when he discovered that not a single Roman would go up and haul down the offending accessories, so Waterton graciously went up a second time and removed them.

5

In 1935 the government of Persia changed the country's name to Iran.

What was Iran called before it was called Persia?

Maybe spinning helps?

Iran ranks third in the world (behind Syria and Turkey) for the number of officially recognized whirling dervishes. Dervishes always spin counter-clockwise. Whether the direction of the whirl expands or decreases colonic capacity has yet to be investigated.

A gassy country?

At the beginning of the present millennium, Iran ranked #2 behind Russia for the planet's largest source of natural gas. But that statistic does not include the vast amounts of colonic gas generated in the country's population by local diets, a trivia fact which may one day become an issue, given Iran's interest in atmospheric research, because like all matter, gas—in the colon and elsewhere—expands in the upper atmosphere. The average human colon, for example, which typically holds about 100 cubic centimeters of gas, can expand as much as seven fold at 30,000 feet (which makes bean and onion casseroles a bad choice before a transcontinental flight).

Testimony to the explosive power of colonic vapors was offered in 1976 by a Minneapolis physician, J.H. Bond, writing in the journal, *Gastrointestinal Endoscopy*. Bond reported that while cauterizing polyps in the colon of a 71 year old male, he (Bond) was blown off his feet and suffered first degree burns from jets of blue flame. Although the doctor recovered naturally, the patient needed surgery.

Iran, its original name. Westerners started calling the area "Persia" centuries ago and the name stuck.

The world changed forever in 1451, when Johannes Gutenberg published 300 copies of the Bible in Mainz, Germany. This was the first printing of a book with movable type.

In what language did he print?

Did William Canton One-Up Gutenberg?

Just 23 years after Gutenberg, William Caxton produced the first movable type publication in English: *The Recuyell of the Histories of Troye*, which he blithely stole from a French manuscript. In the preface, Caxton proudly boasted that the book "is not wreton with penne and ynke as other bokes ben . . . [but was] begonne in oon day and also fynysshid in oon day" (thereby laying claim to being the first printer in history—and possibly the only one—to bring in a print job on time.)

Latin. A pretty small print run, 300 copies, but in publishing it's normal to print small and hope big. Sometimes that works: since Gutenberg the number of Bibles in print numbers in the several billions. Sometimes it doesn't. The first print run of *How to Test Your Urine at Home*, by B.C. Meyrowitz (Haldeman-Julius, 1935), was a paltry 250 copies but never did sell out. Nor did Alfred Rose' *Build Your Own Hindenburg* (Putnam, 1983). On the other hand, all 325 copies of H.V. Cory's *Wall Paintings by Snake Charmers in Tanganyika* (Faber & Faber, 1953) were snapped up in just seven years. And *Recollections of Squatting in Victoria*, by E. Micklethwaite, which hit the shelves in 1883 (500 copies) was reprinted by University of Melbourne Press only 82 years later.

As the song goes, "John Brown's body lies amolderin' in the grave."

Where's the grave?

Going Out—Way Out—In Style?

In 2004, friends of Irish skeet shooter, Jimmy O'Kelly obeyed his dying wish and had his ashes packed into live shotgun shells so they could be shot and scattered over skeet shooting ranges around the world.

How Odd is Odd?

Aimee and John were laid to rest in the traditional face up, horizontal style as are most of our dearly departed. Notable exceptions are former French premier, Georges Clemenceau, who stands upright facing Germany, his old enemy, and Shakespeare's contemporary, Ben Jonson, who has been in a sitting position in Poet's Corner of Westminster Abbey since 1637. These two worthies became *defunctus officio* long before the founding of a support group for this rather unique style. The Society for Perpendicular Internment, got started in Australia in the 1960s and is now world-wide. Mogul emperor Khan Jahan (who built the Taj Mahal) was also ahead of his time. He was buried upright in 1666, but in a special casket with one hand sticking out so his subjects could maintain physical contact, post mortem.

John Brown's grave is in Lake Placid, New York, at John Brown Farm historic site. The headstone comes from his grandfather's grave in Ohio, a request Brown made prior to his execution in 1859 for the famous raid he led on Harper's Ferry. Bit of an odd request perhaps, but not compared to that of Aimee Semple McPherson, founder of the Church of the Foursquare Gospel, who had a telephone installed in her casket when she passed on in 1944.

8

Experts agree it's possible, statistically, for a human to survive being hit by lightning, and are fond of citing the case of R.C. Sullivan of the Virginia Forest Service who made the record books by getting nailed seven times! Sullivan walked away each time . . . well, on a couple of occasions he had to be carried. But he did survive!

ONE UP

If it's possible, statistically, for a human being to survive a hit, then where, statistically, is the safest place to be when lightning strikes?

Does Anybody Really Know?

What science truly knows about lightning is inexact at best. There's no certainty, for example, that lightning rods do any good at all (but just in case, NASA keeps one at the top of the launch gantry). One thing for sure: don't get under a tree. If you need persuading, consider the report of a ranger in Kruger National Park, South Africa, in 1989. He was watching two rhinos mating furiously under a giant baobab tree when lightning struck it, causing a *coitus interruptus* so profound that when the rhinos came to, they forgot the prime objective and wandered away—separately.

Where to take shelter?

In the time it takes to read this page, about six thousand lightning bolts will strike our planet. Not all in the same place, fortunately. The Empire State Building, for example, averages about 100 hits a year, and New York gets a lot fewer thunderstorms than say, Oklahoma City, where tall buildings have been hit as often four times a minute. Far less likely to get a frizz, statistically, is rural North Dakota. Based on available strike data, the Stanford Research Institute estimates that your odds of getting lit up at a Fourth of July picnic in North Dakota—between 3 and 4 p.m.—are a million to one against.

Anywhere but at home, it seems.

The stats show that over half the victims of lightning strikes were indoors. On the other hand, Mr. Sullivan took all his hits outside so really, who knows?

9

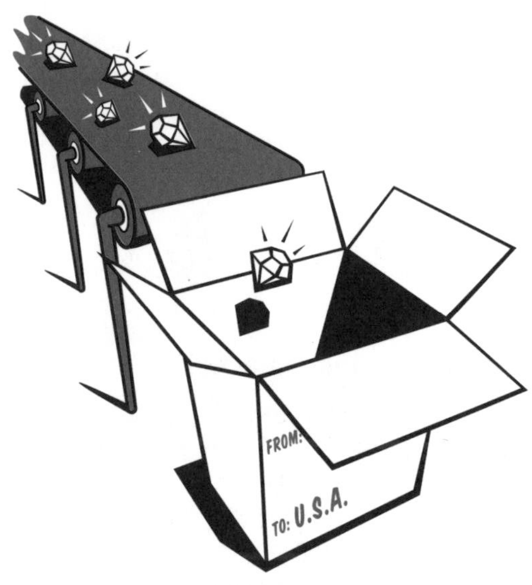

The U.S.A. is the world's largest consumer of diamonds.

What country is the world's largest producer of diamonds?

Where Is the World's Most Beautiful Diamond?

While the Cullinan is—or was before it was cut up—the biggest diamond, gemologists rank The Florentine as the most beautiful. The Florentine is—or was—138 carats, and light yellow with green overtones. It was supposedly picked off the body of Charles the Bold of Burgundy after a battle in 1467, and sold as a piece of glass by a common soldier. Pope Julius II is one of several supposed former owners, but its true provenance begins with the Medicis in the 1650s. Political marriages moved it around Europe until it ended up with the Austrian royal family about 1740. They took it into exile in Switzerland in 1919, after which it has never been seen again.

What of South Africa?

Still a major producer, but not like the old days when it had a wrap on both production and fantastic finds, a prime example of the latter being the famed Cullinan Diamond. It was the largest diamond in the world, discovered when a miner tripped over it near Pretoria in 1905. Over 100 stones were cut from the Cullinan after it was mailed (yes!) to England, one of which is the 530 carat Star of Africa, now part of the British Crown Jewels. You can see that stone at the Tower of London.

Russia.

However, that's according to *Pravda*, a Russian journal that has never won an award for accuracy. Diamond production numbers are hard to nail down, but Botswana seems to be in second place, with Canada now accepted by the industry as third in global production and moving up. Australia and India are in close pursuit.

CATEGORY 3

Headlines

BREAKING NEWS
BREAK

“Prominent Local Bicycle Merchants to be Home for Christmas”

That’s how a Dayton, Ohio newspaper led off an article about the Wright brothers in December, 1903. Readers who persevered beyond the first paragraph were also told that Wilbur and Orville were in North Carolina at the time, experimenting with a flying machine.

We all know that Wilbur and Orville nailed a historic first flight at Kitty Hawk on December 17, 1903. In fact, they got up four times that day.

Which brother went up first?

Other historic aviation firsts?

Charles Lindbergh, of course: not the first person to cross the Atlantic non-stop, in fact the eighty-first, but he was first to do it solo (in 1927). The first Atlantic non-stop belongs to John Alcock and Arthur Brown, who crossed in 1919.

Then there's Luftwaffe Major Rudolf Schenk. He was flying a Heinkel 280, on January 13, 1942 and became the first pilot to safely use an ejection seat in a real emergency.

The first in-flight meals were served on the London-Paris run in 1919 by the Hadley-Page airline service.

The first aerial propaganda campaign was carried out by the Italian air service in January, 1912. Italy was at war with Turkey and dropped leaflets offering a gold coin and a sack of barley to any Turkish soldiers who surrendered.

Somewhat less creative by comparison was a KLM first in 1935. The airline offered the world's first giveaway flight bags—but only on their Amsterdam-Jakarta flight and you had to fly the whole route to get one.

The most important flying first of all? The world's first airplane toilet was test flown (and flushed) on a Russian Vitiaz, May 13, 1913.

Orville. He covered about 120 feet in that first flight. In the fourth, Wilbur flew 852. Still, whether the Wrights were really first is moot. In 1890, Frenchman Clement Ader flew his steam-powered Eole a distance of 164 feet (Wright fans call this a "hop" and dismiss it on that basis).

2

Although most people have trouble coming up with the title of this song, just about anyone can finish its best known line: "He's the man who broke the bank at . . ." Sure, Monte Carlo. The man who inspired the song and the international headlines that went with it was British gambler Charles Deville, and although he didn't really break the bank at Monte Carlo, he had a heck of a run.

What was he playing?

How's This for Odds?

For thirty-one years Doreen Burley lovingly polished and fondled a brass trinket she'd bought at a boutique in Bradford, England, even dropping it on occasion. In 1988 a stranger at her door, with expertise in bomb disposal, recognized it for what it was.

And yes, it was live.

Roulette: a good choice?

So-so. Today's wheels pay out at a rate of 95% which is not bad but less than craps which, according to Consumers Research Magazine, is 98%. Racetracks average 83-87% over a season, and jai lai about the same. Slots range from 95% down to 75% (despite the claims of casinos) and lotteries sport a lousy rate of 49%. Whether or not these odds correlate with luck or brain power is debatable. A California anti-gambling group once successfully taught a chimpanzee to play the slots (she lost her stake). The same chimp won at craps and roulette, but couldn't figure out race track betting. And she never bought a lottery ticket, a somewhat more intelligent move than that of a Montreal holdup man in 1976. In addition to grabbing cash during a robbery he scooped a pile of unsold lottery tickets, one of which, at the end of the week, turned out to be such a big winner he came out of hiding to collect. He made parole in 1982.

Roulette. Back in 1873 Deville sat down at the wheel with a few hundred dollars and cashed out with $325,000. No big deal in today's world, but better than losing, and he quit while he was ahead!

3

"Disgusting Machine Invented by German Physicist"

The English daily, *The Pall Mall Gazette*, made this declaration in 1895, when editors learned that a device invented by Wilhelm Roentgen produced mysterious rays that could pass through flesh and take pictures of bones. Roentgen called his discovery "X-Rays."

What does the "X" stand for?

How Did "X" Become a Symbol for Kissing

"X" became a symbol for a kiss because illiterate people who could not sign their names would inscribe an X and then kiss it as a kind of guarantee.

It doesn't stand for anything—because Roentgen wasn't really sure what he had discovered and didn't know what to call it.

Despite praise from the scientific community (Roentgen got the first ever Nobel for physics), others were considerably less enthusiastic. By 1900, an English clothing manufacturer was advertising "X-Ray-proof clothing for naturally modest ladies." In New Jersey, the government introduced a bill to forbid X-rays in opera glasses. And Roentgen's wife never went near the machine again after she saw the bones in her hand.

The experience of pharmacist Max Kiss with "X" was somewhat different. Among Max's best customers were several winemakers and over time, Max noticed that whenever he sold them phenolphthalein (to check the acidity of their wines) the subsequent taste test would bring on a mild case of the trots the next day. Being sensitive to the ghastly reputation of popular laxatives like castor oil, Max hit upon the idea of adding phenolphthalein to chocolate. The result was a pleasant tasting motivator and in 1905 he began to market it under the unfortunate brand name of Bo-Bo. As a sales venture it was a total dud and he would have given up had it not been for an acquaintance who observed that his concoction was an "excellent laxative." For Max, it was an easy step from Bo-Bo to Ex-Lax.

"They're Back!"

It's the biggest event of the year in Capistrano and every March 19 or so it inspires headlines, because that's when the swallows return. And it has been happening for hundreds of years. Every year in March the swallows come back to Capistrano.

Where have they been?

Why do Parachutes Come Without Guarantees?

The first recorded use of a parachute in wartime had an equally dubious outcome. Hans Weimer of the German Air Service bailed out of his Albatross DVa in April 1918—right over the British trenches in Belgium. He was shot twenty-seven times before touching the ground.

In Argentina. Around the town of Goya, to be specific—although to our knowledge there is no song with the title, "When the Swallows Come Back to Goya." They come back from Capistrano in late October.

Usually the birds in Capistrano are outnumbered by tourists, all of them clustered together and looking up—which forces speculation as to whether these people have thought about the consequences of gathering underneath large numbers of feathered creatures whose bodies process food in the usual manner.

Such thoughts did not occur to a crowd of Frenchmen who, in 1797, gathered to watch André-Jacques Garnerin make the world's first parachute descent (from a hot air balloon). Garnerin landed safely, but his design was still in the experimental stages and the parachute oscillated wildly on the way down, making him so seasick he threw up on his cheering countrymen below.

5

"Russian Cosmonaut Orbits Earth"

His name was Yuri Gagarin and in 1961 he orbited the planet in a spacecraft, adding yet another to the string of "firsts" claimed by the Russian space program. America's astronauts, however, can claim a "first" or two of their own.

Who is the first person to orbit Earth on a toilet seat?

Who needs this?

The U.S. *Gemini* space program in the 1960s was especially plagued with the floating results of failed waste storage systems. Case in point: when the first navy frogman reached the floating capsule of *Gemini 7* after splashdown in the Pacific, he opened the hatch, looked in, and promptly passed out.

U.S. astronaut Pete Conrad.

In 1973, Conrad sat on the can for 90 minutes, the length of time it took for Skylab space station to make a single orbit of the planet. It was a personal project (not necessarily cleared in advance with NASA) and he had his fellow astronauts on Skylab verify the time, not to mention the activity. Gagarin's orbit of Earth took a bit longer, 108 minutes, but since his Vostok did not have an *en suite*, it's likely he made a point of going before he went.

Although American and Soviet space programs competed neck and neck for over thirty years, neither one came close to a satisfactory solution to outer space potty problems. In the early days, when short flights were the norm, the crew just gritted their teeth, but as flights lengthened, they were forced into designer diapers. Eventually, however, engineers simply had to come up with a working toilet for flights lasting over several days. Not an easy task. Because of weightlessness, there simply is no "plop!" And storage is an even worse problem (which may explain why giant pandas are unlikely to be used for experimental flights any time soon; they go about 48 times a day!)

6

"Doctor Livingstone, I presume?"

All the world thought famed explorer David Livingstone had died somewhere in the interior of darkest Africa. Then on November 10, 1871, journalist Henry Stanley found him on the shores of Lake Tanganyika, and scored what is quite possibly the best-known greeting of all time.

What did Livingstone reply?

Ever Feel this Way?

Livingstone may not have known it, but his recurring hemorrhoids are an affliction shared by many. Karl Marx, Alfred the Great, and Napoleon were sufferers, as is Elizabeth Taylor. Slugger George Brett of the Kansas City Royals played through the 1980 World Series with a bad case. Every time he came to bat the cameras focused on his butt.

"Yes." Okay, not a bell ringer, but Livingstone was hardly in the mood for sound bites, being somewhat preoccupied with a bout of malaria aggravated by dysentery and severe arthritis, not to mention lacerated eyes from a whipped branch and deafness from rheumatic fever. He'd also lost the use of his left arm in a lion attack just a short time before, and was suffering from a killer case of hemorrhoids. It's hard to think of a memorable quip in these conditions.

Livingstone was more than a bit surprised to be "found," because he knew exactly where he was. But *The New York Herald*, which sponsored Stanley's search, would have none of that, and turned the meeting—and Stanley's greeting—into a world-wide headline. As for Stanley, the event seemed to develop a bug in him for finding other people who weren't lost, either. In 1885, he "found" Emin Pasha, the governor of Sudan, who had tripped off for some extended relaxation in the mountains of the Congo. The Pasha (who was, in fact, a minor German noble named Edward Schnitzer that had conned his way into upgraded status in North Africa) was having a perfectly agreeable time in the Congo and wasn't much interested in being "found."

7

"Mr. Watson, come here! I want to see you!"

As famous as they are, these words never actually became a headline. They were spoken by Alexander Graham Bell in his laboratory and were carried over wires to his assistant, Thomas Watson.

Why did Bell want him?

Do all Inventions Cause a Spat?

While Bell was fighting off lawsuits (over 600), another tinkerer, Joseph Cowan, had developed the electric flowerpot, a tube with battery and bulb designed to illuminate flowers. It worked fine but commercially was a bust, so Cowan sold rights to an employee, Conrad Hubert. Hubert modified the design, took aim at a different market, and founded the Eveready Flashlight Company. Cowan wasn't the least bit upset, because by then he was totally absorbed in developing toy electric trains. Unlike the electric flowerpot venture, his trains became a huge commercial success. (Cowan's middle name was Lionel.)

Who Else Invented the Telephone?

Italian-Americans believe, with good reason, that the real inventor of the telephone is Antonio Meucci, who emigrated to New York in 1850, but who had neither the sophistication nor the money to support his own invention against Bell and his backers. The most familiar "other inventor" is Oberlin professor Elisha Gray, who walked into the patent office in Boston with his telephone invention, only two hours after Bell had filed.

But was it really the first call?

In Europe, Bell's achievement is regarded as just another "stolen by America" myth, because on that continent the first telephone call is credited to Johann Philipp Reis, a clear fifteen years earlier. Reis first demonstrated his phone to the Physical Society of Frankfurt in 1861, and then in many countries of Europe (including Scotland, where some historians believe Bell witnessed a demonstration).

He had spilled acid on his crotch and wanted help, thereby making the first telephone call the first 9-1-1 as well.

8

Mention Mrs. O'Leary's cow and it's an easy leap to the Chicago Fire. According to the headlines, on the evening of October 8, 1871, her cow kicked over a lantern in the barn at 137 De Koven Street, starting a blaze that took 250 lives.

What happened to the cow?

More from Sarah?

Among Sarah Hale's more provocative feminist claims is denial that the sexes are equal. God created the earth and its creatures, she pointed out, in ascending order with Eve, the final pinnacle of accomplishment. (Hale ignores Eve's well-known failure in the Garden of Eden.)

Did Mary Have a Little Lamb?

The nursery rhyme appeared in 1830 in a book of poetry by uber-feminist Sarah Hale. The Mary of the poem was little Mary Sawyer, whose pet lamb followed her to school one day, an event that inspired a visiting student minister to write the poem, which Hale then published. At least that's what the folks in Sterling, Massachusetts believe (they have a statue to prove it), and so did Henry Ford I, who moved the school building—complete with the front lawn—to his grand museum at Greenfield, Michigan. Revisionists, however, prefer to suggest that poems like these had been popular for centuries as Bible instruction for children. (E.g., Mary, the Virgin, had a lamb, Jesus, who as an innocent child, would go everywhere that Mary went.) Still, it's more fun to believe than scoff.

It survived, which is appropriate, because the animal was innocent.

The fire did indeed start in the O'Leary's barn, but a Chicago newspaper reporter, Michael Ahern, confessed he made up the lantern bit. Lovers of tall tales, dismayed by the lack of truth in this famous cow story, seek reassurance in the certainty that farther east, in Massachusetts, Mary did indeed have a little lamb that followed her to school one day, but even this story has loopholes.

"Prince Rainier Marries Grace Kelly"

That was in Monaco in 1956, a busy year around the world. Nasser seized the Suez Canal in Egypt. *My Fair Lady* opened in New York. Fidel Castro landed with a small force in Cuba in 1956. Martin Luther King Jr. began a boycott in Alabama.

What did Warwick Kerr do in Brazil?

Is There Bee Stuff You Should Know?

Bees operate on the principle of "Don't-mess-with-me-and-I-won't-mess-with-you," but in case you run into some that have not read the manual, you should know they chase dark things rather than light, so don't wear your Boston Bruins home ice sweater when poking under the eaves. Once bees attack, the best defense is retreat. Their top speed is 12–15 mph, slower than most humans so running away is effective. But run far enough; killer bees will chase for up to a quarter mile. And don't jump into the pool. They wait for you to come up for air.

Since Kerr's time, researchers have learned that after copulating with the queen, a drone's testicles explode with an audible pop. (He dies, too, but the other result, unfortunately, comes first.) Not that this information helps if you're being chased; besides, drones only chase the queen.

He gave us killer bees. In 1956, Kerr launched a project crossbreeding native (and stingless) Brazilian bees with a very aggressive African strain. The following year, some of his research subjects escaped, 26 swarms to be precise, and by 1993 had claimed their first victim in the lower 48. Not as bad as Brazil, where authorities have attributed over 300 fatalities to these "Africanized honey bees." Indeed, in 1973 they actually laid siege to the town of Recife. Local citizens had to lock themselves indoors, while asbestos-clad firefighters took on the attackers with flamethrowers.

CATEGORY

4

Sports

GO TEAM!

Basketball is played on a court, golf on a course, baseball on a field, boxing in a ring, ping-pong on a table.

Where is kittenball played?

A catcher's nightmare, too?

Barehanded catchers of the day suffered from overhand pitching until the "puff pillow mitt" invented by Harry Decker restored some comfort. Yet this big mitt has led to over-confidence on occasion, Joe "No Teeth" Sprinz, of the Cleveland Indians being a case in point. For a pregame publicity stunt in 1939, Sprintz agreed to catch a baseball dropped from a plane at 1000 feet. Whether he was unaware of the laws of gravity or chose to ignore them is not known, but he made the catch with the mitt held just above his face.

A Batter's Nightmare?

In 1884, big league baseball switched from underhand to overhand pitching without repositioning the pitcher's mound (just fifty feet from home plate at the time), and the game turned boring. Strikeout numbers soared and action on the field dropped to near zero. (In the 1885 season, Hugh Daily, a one-armed pitcher for Boston of the Union Association League racked up 483 k's!) It took big league baseball until 1893 to fix things by moving the pitcher's mound to its present day distance of 60' 6" from home plate.

"Kittenball" is the name the Farragut Boat Club of Chicago chose in 1887 when they developed what would eventually be called "softball" (but not officially until 1926). Kittenball, with underhand pitching, was an instant, popular alternative to baseball or "hardball," because the grand old game had become hard to play.

2

Marathon races commemorate a heroic dash in 490 B.C. by a Greek courier (legend says it was Pheidippides), who ran from Marathon to Athens to announce the defeat of the Persians. From Marathon to Athens is about 26 miles. The modern Olympic marathon is 26 miles, 385 yards.

Where do the extra 385 yards come from?

Is There a Medal for Meddling?

The original (a.k.a. 'ancient') Olympics had its share of manipulation too. Prime example: in 66 CE, Emperor Nero competed in the chariot race, the hot event of the time. Officials had to restart the race several times until other competitors finally caught on and let him win. There was no marathon in the original Olympics; the longest foot race was about three miles. Nero won that one too in 66, as well as several events that he made up on the spot. Emperors can do that of course, but not all of them behave that way. Emperor Theodosius abolished the Olympics in 394 CE as too commercialized, no longer for amateurs, and corrupt.

The 1908 Olympics in London, England.

Organizers added a lap around the stadium so runners would finish in front of Queen Alexandra in the royal box. Somehow the added yardage stuck. The change that year caused far less flap than the event itself. Crowd favorite Dorando Pietri of Italy was leading, but once in the stadium he ran the wrong way. His handlers turned him around, but then he collapsed. They revived him and he went down again, so they carried him across the finish line. Despite a near riot in the crowd, he was disqualified—just like American Fred Lorz four years before. At the 1904 games in St. Louis, Lorz was first across the line and had already been presented with the gold, when it was discovered he'd ridden half the route in a car!

3

Hockey fans know that Lorne "Gump" Worsley played goal for the New York Rangers.

What did Gladys Goodding play for the New York Rangers?

A High Risk Cup?

Lord Stanley also never learned that his cup was used as a flowerpot in 1907 by the wife of the Ottawa Silver Sevens' photographer (she didn't know what it was); or that it was left by the side of the road in 1924 (its courier stopped to change a flat tire). The cup has been carried to the top of Mount Elbert in Colorado, and was once dropkicked into the Rideau Canal. It has appeared with Jay Leno and David Letterman, and has been a guest of both Bill Clinton and Vladimir Putin. Only once was it stolen: from Chicago Stadium, by a Montreal Canadiens fan who couldn't bear to see it there.

What Is the Oldest Trophy in Professional Sport?

The Stanley Cup has been presented every year since 1893, making it the oldest trophy for professional sport in North America. The New York Rangers (first season: 1926-27) have won it four times, and Gladys was around to play the organ for two of those. That's two more than Lord Stanley, the Canadian governor-general who first donated the cup. He was recalled to England just before the 1893 series, and as a result, never got to see a Stanley Cup game.

The organ. Gladys had a long tenure at Madison Square Gardens, playing at Knicks' games, too. She had special songs for visiting teams: "Chicago" for the Blackhawks, "Pretty Red Wing" for Detroit, and "Saskatchewan" for the Toronto Maple Leafs, even though Toronto is nowhere near the Canadian province of Saskatchewan!

When you think of women tennis stars, the name Maud Watson doesn't spring to the lips as quickly as, say, Billie Jean King, or Serena and Venus Williams, but Maud is right up there in the record books. In 1884 she became the first—ever winner of women's singles at Wimbledon.

Another not-so-well-known professional tennis player owns a Wimbledon first too: Lily de Alvarez. What did Lily do in 1931 to earn her spot?

Does Gender Matter?

Less animate than Anne or Maud or Lily, but definitely feminine is *Liberty Enlightening the World*, the proper name of the Statue of Liberty in New York Harbor. *Liberty* is one of only a very few female statues world-wide. The prejudice that produces only male statues goes all the way back to classical Greece, a bias that should have at least established male anatomical accuracy early on, but that is not the case. On nude male statues, early Greek sculptors habitually portrayed the testicles as equals. Not until about 480 BCE, it seems, did they check before chipping, and make the right one smaller and higher.

Another Feminine First?

Anne, the Princess Royal, eldest daughter of Queen Elizabeth II, holds a double first in Olympic competition, neither of which, sadly, has a medal to go with it. Anne was the first British princess to become an Olympic contestant (Montreal '76; equestrian events). She was also the first competitor to have the chromosome test (to prove gender) waived.

Play in shorts. Snorts of disapproval echoed on both sides of the Atlantic, but Lily stuck to her . . . well, shorts. No slouch player, this was Lily's fourth trip to the finals, but in 1931 she was not only past her prime, she also had the bad luck to face Helen Wills. Since the first Wimbledon in 1884, when Maud triumphed, the only woman to win more singles crowns than Helen Wills is Martina Navratilova.

5

Sportscasters outside of the U.S. who report on the NFL call the NFL game "*American* football." (Most of the time they just ignore it.) In turn, when American sportscasters report on football in the other continents they call the local game "soccer."

To be correct, what should Americans be calling the foreign games?

One Shared Element?

All football leagues around the world agree that unnecessary rough play should be penalized. (This does not cover shooting the referee, as has happened more than once in Latin America.) The U.S. game in particular added provisos against rough play in 1906, when President Teddy Roosevelt, no powder puff himself, threatened to abolish football altogether because it was too rough. He may have been motivated by the comment of a French tourist who, after seeing his first game, wondered "if this is playing, it is impossible to tell what they might call fighting."

Was it always like this?

Yes, if the first McGill-Harvard series is typical. In 1874, the McGill University team in Montreal accepted Harvard's challenge to play the first known international game of "football." As soon as the ball was snapped it was clear the teams played by different rules. To complete the game officials tried both sets of rules, but in the end nobody changed. Nearly a century and a half later, Canadian football still has twelve-man teams on a bigger field and far more backfield motion.

Football, or to be absolutely precise, "association football."

The U.S. is the only country that plays "American football," while "football" is played in over 140 countries in six continents. Not that this more popular game is without variation, as other countries also offer versions like rugby, Gaelic football, Australian football, and Canadian football.

Even if you aren't a golfer, you have probably heard of a "mulligan," an outside-the-rules, do-again shot that friendly golfers agree on to take the place of one badly done.

Where does the name "mulligan" come from?

Where Does the Word "Golf" Come From?

The origin of the word "golf" attracts its own share of myth. One dead wrong claim is that the word is an acronym for "gentlemen only, ladies forbidden," a popular belief. More probable but still unproven is that the word comes from the Netherlands. Dutch people played *kolven* with a *kolf* (club) on frozen canals (putting must have been interesting), and the game is said to have migrated to Scotland in the 1500s, where it was called *gowf* (and was taken up by such fans as Mary, Queen of Scots, who drew sharp criticism when she was seen getting a game in the day after her first husband was strangled).

Unknown. Theories abound, however, and a popular one attributes the origin to an individual named Mulligan. Not a bad idea, but was it David Mulligan of the St. Lambert Club in Quebec, or Buddy Mulligan of the Essex Fells Club in New Jersey? Both are cited by the USGA Museum—along with the caveat that there's no proof for either man. Another theory slams the Irish. As they tried to elevate themselves socially in the late nineteenth century, the premise goes, they turned to golf as a genteel game, but they were such duffers they always needed extra shots. Yet another postulation puts the origin in Irish saloons, where the publican would keep a bottle to give free extras to his friends.

7

In a sport obsessed with records, one stat continues to sit atop the pile despite its increasing age: in 1961, Yankees outfielder Roger Maris hit 61 home runs and broke the record set by Babe Ruth in 1927.

Whose record did Ruth break?

Maris Forgotten?

Despite being MVP for two consecutive years prior to the big 1961 year, Roger Maris always played under the shadow of Mickey Mantle. It didn't help, either, that the following season Maris had to struggle to meet half of his home run production of the year before. As if to offer a final insult, for years *The Guinness Book of World Records* dutifully published his accomplishment, but listed him in the wrong league.

Record Man Ruth?

No other slugger ever came close to Babe Ruth's pitching prowess. From 1917 to 1960, when Whitey Ford caught up to him, Ruth held the World Series record for consecutive scoreless innings pitched. He also set the scene for a record that still sits on the books. In 1917, pitching for the Boston Red Sox, Ruth walked the first batter on four pitches. His response to that shortcoming was to punch out umpire Brick Owens, for which, quite naturally, he was ejected. Teammate Ernie Shore came in to throw the only perfect game, thus far, by a reliever.

His own. Ruth hit 59 dingers in 1921, positively shattering a record held until then by long-forgotten third baseman Roger Connor, who played in the National League from 1880 to 1896. In 1887, while playing for the recently renamed New York Giants—they had been the Gothams before—Connor hit 17 home runs, a season high that held up for 34 years.

The five interlocking rings of the International Olympics are a well-known logo. You've seen the rings many times, and you know the colors: blue, black, yellow, green and red.

Why those colors?

Medals for the other End?

If the Olympics ever awarded medals for being inept, there's little doubt that at the 1960 Summer Games in Rome, the gold would have gone to the pentathlon team from Tunisia. In the first pentathlon event, the riding competition, every member of the Tunisian team fell off his horse, thus becoming the first contestants in the history of the Games to score zero in an event. In the pool they came last because several members couldn't swim (one had to rescued). The team was disqualified in the fencing competition. Only one could fence and he was sent out three times. (For the third match he forgot to put his mask on in time.) During the pistol shooting they were ordered off the range when one of them nearly plinked a judge. Only in cross-country running did they finish without a fault—but came in last.

Tunisia's flag, incidentally, is red and white.

At least one of the colors appears in every national flag (except for the flags of Qatar and Latvia, where you have to really use your imagination). The colors have proven to be a more enduring choice than some Olympic events. For example, we no longer get to see croquet, club swinging, throwing the javelin with two hands, rope climbing, dueling pistols (!), and what must have been a heck of a crowd-pleaser: "plunging"—floating the longest distance in sixty seconds after a standing dive. These were all medal events in 1904.

"The Masters" has been a yearly event since 1934. The "Benson & Hedges Masters" has been a yearly event since 1975.

"The Masters" is a golf tournament. What sport does the "Benson & Hedges Masters" celebrate?

All about image?

Despite the high degree of skill required of champions in traditional pool, that game has long suffered from an image of low-level hustling in smoke-filled rooms. The premier players often used names that reinforced this perception, names like Wimpy Lassiter and Jersey Red, and the inimitable Rodolfe Wonderone Jr., better known as "Minnesota Fats." Snooker, on the other hand, is played by royalty. It was the Maharajah of Cooch Behar who first introduced the game to the British officer class in the 1880s, and these worthies brought it home to gentleman's clubs in Europe. The very thought of hustling would have made them shudder.

Snooker. The B&H was never a ranking tournament—of which there are nine throughout Europe. Because of England's tobacco laws, the Benson & Hedges Tobacco Company is no longer the sponsor, but the B&H, still called that by aficionados, is *the* tournament in the game. Granted, the purse at golf's great tournament in Augusta, Georgia, is considerably higher than what the top snooker player walks away with in Preston, England, but then snooker players don't have to tip caddies or rent carts, and they can keep playing during a thunderstorm. Not that snooker winners are exactly on the dole (the English welfare system). Canadian Cliff Thorburn (so far the only non-Brit winner) who has taken the trophy three times, was retained after his first win by the Sultan of Brunei to teach snooker to his sons at $3,000 an hour.

CATEGORY

5

The Natural World

1

A dog of mixed pedigree is called a "mongrel."

What do you call a cat with a mixed pedigree?

Feline Inspiration?

Frederic Chopin was moved to compose "Waltz No. 3 in F" when a cat walked across his piano. Cats are pacers and it was this gait, Chopin said, which inspired him. Camels and giraffes are pacers, too, and one cannot help but wonder what Chopin might have composed if one of these had walked over his piano instead.

More Than One Kind of Cat?

The original settlers of Australia (convicts) were all too familiar with another cat, the "cat o'nine tails" used for floggings, especially in eighteenth-century navies. The term "cat" came from the scratches left behind by barbs attached to the nine tails of a whip.

When erect, a male cat's penis also has such barbs, but this is probably not what inspired the navies to add them to whips, because these hooks on a tomcat's *organus erectus* were not discovered—by humans anyway—until the twentieth century. Biologists explain that since cats often copulate in a hurry, the extra appendage makes it easier to get a grip, as it were. In any case, female cats (properly called "queens") don't seem to be bothered by the hook, so much so that it is quite common for a queen to entertain several toms in a single session (which goes a long way toward explaining why there are so many moggies). Such group adventures, incidentally, are known to biologists as "superfecundation," although other terms spring to mind.

A moggy. Australians claim they invented the term in a hit novelty song, "He's Nobody's Moggy Now," expressing delight over a road kill, but the word was used in England well before the first Europeans made it down under.

2

When the great Secretariat won the Triple Crown in 1973, breaking track records for all three races, he stood 16.2 hands tall.

How big is a "hand"?

What's in a (Horse) Name?

Roy Rogers' "Trigger" (15.3 hands) is arguably the best-known horse ever, although when Trigger's movie career started he was a no-name. The Lone Ranger's "Silver" (16.3) began that way too, but he got bragging rights by carrying Scarlett O'Hara's father in all of his riding scenes in *Gone with the Wind*. In *The Godfather*, the gruesomely decapitated horse was "Khartoum." In Imperial Russia, everyone knew "Krepysh" was the favorite mount of Czar Nicholas II, which may explain why Krepysh was publicly executed by a Bolshevik firing squad in 1919. In the Third Reich, German farmers were forbidden to name a horse "Adolf." The Führer's name was also an official no-no on mountains, roses, churches, and butter tarts.

Four inches. A horse's height is measured from the ground to the top of the withers, the high point between the front shoulders. Secretariat, therefore, was 64.8 inches tall. Big, but even with head held high, he'd have come in way under the world record holder, Mammoth, an English Shire horse who topped out at 21.5 hands (86 inches) in 1846. Mammoth also weighed about twice as much as an adult moose.

Seabiscuit by comparison was small, just 15.2 hands, but in the 2003 movie about this wonderful horse his stand-ins are somewhat taller. But then the movie made other adjustments, too. Like flags. In the Pimlico racetrack sequence, which shows how Seabiscuit became a legend in 1938 by winning a match race against Triple Crown winner War Admiral (18 hands), the Maryland flag is upside down while the U.S. flag has 50 stars, thereby granting statehood to Alaska and Hawaii two decades early.

3

Say "paparazzi" to your favorite trivia buff and you'll be told it's an Italian word for the hordes of aggressive photographers who surround a celebrity at every turn.

What does "paparazzi" mean in Italian?

Is There Hope?

What may save us all one day is the discovery of San Diego guitarist Robert Brown. In 1972, despite a steady round of complaints from his neighbors, he was able to verify that repeated riffs from his Gibson Flying V at maximum volume would actually kill cockroaches. Not mosquitoes, unfortunately, although there was an unforeseen side benefit: a family of rats abandoned the basement apartment where Brown's trials were conducted.

Only Female Mosquitoes Bite. True?

Yes, but less widely known is that most varities have 47 teeth and that humans who are fair-skinned, blonde, and eat garlic are primary targets. Such high levels of scientific awareness have done much to position the mosquito even lower than the cockroach on the scale of insect appreciation.

Mosquitoes. A pesky freelance photographer in the 1959 Frederico Fellini film, *La Dolce Vita*, was called "Paparazzo," and that's how it all started.

Just like celebrity photographers, there are about 1500 varieties of mosquito in the world. They swarm polar bears in Greenland, snakes in Brazil, camels in Syria, and even go after fish. European explorers in North America developed special curses for them, and early missionaries couldn't accept that they were actually God's creatures.

In the animal kingdom, few critters leave a more lasting and regrettable effect than skunks, which makes them one of the most avoided species of all.

Do skunks gross out other skunks?

Does It Get Worse?

Mercaptan is an oily, greenish fluid produced in a pair of musk sacs and discharged through the anus. (If you wonder who spends the time to figure this out, consider the career of chemist Hennig Brand, who discovered phosphorus in 1699 while investigating the properties of urine.) Finally, skunks eat just about anything but go absolutely nuts over raw eggs. Biologists estimate your chances of attracting skunks go up several hundred per cent if you raise chickens, so don't keep them on the patio on summer nights.

No. A skunk's first level of warning to any intruder—even your dog when it's dumb enough to claim rights to the back yard—is to thump its paws on the ground. Other skunks usually get this message quickly. A second level is lifting its tail and aiming it. Only if these fail does it opt for spray, but even then, only if it feels it has to. (However, you shouldn't depend on all this sequence every time; skunks are not I.Q. leaders in the animal world.)

Skunk facts to reflect on after it's too late: Spray range is up to twelve feet and a healthy adult can spray up to six times in an encounter, albeit with diminishing power. Striped skunks, the most common, have to point their butt in the right direction, but spotted skunks are actually capable of a brief handstand from which position they can spray forward. The spray is a sulphide called mercaptan, the active chemical being ethanethiol. Humans—not a species noted for having good noses—can pick up the smell of mercaptan up to two miles away. In fact, under laboratory conditions, a human can detect ethanethiol at one part in ten trillion!

5

Mice get together in "hordes," "nests," and "mischiefs." Rats, too, gather in hordes, nests and mischiefs, and in "colonies," "packs," "plagues," and "swarms." The gender names of mice are "buck" for the male and "doe" for the female.

What are the gender names for rats?

And smart?

In yet another experiment, this one at Cambridge University, 87.5 per cent of a swarm, when given a choice, regularly picked cheese over a Mars bar.

But Cultured?

Researchers at University College in Cardiff, Wales, demonstrated that rats are not only sensitive to music, but even show a preference. Their experimental group lined up to hear Mozart piano concertos . . . and stayed away from acid rock.

Just How Tough Are Rats?

Rats can scale brick walls, tread water for up to three days (so much for the phrase "drowned rat"), eat through lead pipe or cinder blocks, and in experiments carried out while animal rights activists were looking the other way, researchers found that rats can survive a five-story drop about 80% of the time. If threatened they will attack anything of any size, and they also have great staying power, being able, for example, to survive without water longer than a camel.

Male rat and female rat. Although their offspring are known as "pups" or sometimes as "pinkies"—especially by people who find them cuddly—their parents do not seem to merit their own name. Strange for a species whose population on the planet is believed to match that of humans.

6

"Sweat like a horse" is a phrase you've certainly heard. And horses do sweat. So do cows and sheep. Apes are particularly sweaty and even hippopotamuses do it. (Their sweat is red!) You don't usually hear someone say "sweat like a hippopotamus" though, or "sweat like an ape," but you often hear "sweat like a pig."

Do pigs sweat?

As for the rest of us . . .

Humans rank close to the top of the animal heap when it comes to sweating, with the typical male of our species exuding at rate double of that of the typical female (except during menopausal flashes). Camels, on the other hand, are like pigs in that they hardly sweat at all. But they are very unlike pigs when it comes to choosing their potty spots. Which may explain why camels are usually led, not driven.

So what's with the sweat?

Unfortunately the inability to sweat through their skin makes them victims of internal thermodynamics and they can become living proof that too much heat scrambles the brains. At temperatures over 84°F pigs seem to lose it so badly that when it comes to defecation, well, the floor's the limit.

Clean as a pig?

When pigs are penned up, they are careful to go potty in a designated area (different from smokers in that with pigs, the designated area is voluntary). The area is well away from where they eat and sleep—or wallow. It's a group-monitored behavior and because, like all animal species, pigs have slower learners in their midst, it's quite common to see them body-blocking one of their number into the chosen spot if they see him or her about to commit a social disgrace.

No. They are very susceptible to sunburn, but the reason they wallow in mud has more to do with lack of perspiration than lack of sunblock. Unfortunately, the wallowing habit has led to bad press like "dirty as a pig" and "lazy as a pig." Only the "lazy" epithet comes close to the truth because given a chance, pigs will actually keep themselves pretty clean.

7

Television's most-loved horse—well, most-loved *talking* horse—was Mr. Ed, the handsome palamino on the sitcom of the same name. The show began with the theme song, "A horse is a horse, of course, of course," which of course it is. And a cow is a cow, a dog is a dog and a squirrel is a squirrel.

Is a toad a toad?

Frog Power?

During an eclipse of the moon over Cambodia in 1972, the ruling Khmer Rouge feared the moon was being attacked by the monster frog, Reahou (a Cambodian bogeyman), and ordered an entire regiment of infantry to fire at the sky. When the smoke cleared there were over fifty casualties among the armed forces and two innocent civilians were shot.

The moon, however, was saved.

Mark Twain, a plagiarist?

Every American school kid knows Mark Twain launched his literary career with "The Celebrated Jumping Frog of Calaveras County" in 1865. What the kids usually don't know is that the story actually comes from Greece and is over two thousand years old. The good news is Twain didn't know either, so the plagiarism was probably innocent. The Calaveras hero, by the way, was a California red-legged frog, once believed to be extinct, but a pond full was discovered in 2003.

Actually, it's a type of frog. Should you find this disconcerting, however, there are ways to distinguish frogs from toads. The latter lay their eggs in clumps, while frogs prefer strings. Toads have thicker skins, thicker soles and, according to a carefully constructed investigation by some Canadian biologists, tend to be right-handed (okay, right-footed), unlike much of the animal kingdom—where right-left preference is fairly evenly distributed.

As far back as the 1850s, U.S. businessmen were making a fortune out of bat poop, mining it from caves in Peru where, after a night of flying and foraging, millions of bats would hang upside-down during the daylight hours. Which begs the question . . .

How do bats poop if they are hanging upside down?

And Millard Fillmore . . . ?

America's 13th president is frequently described by his critics as only marginally more active than the order *Chiroptera* in daytime, but the fact is President Fillmore once played a crucial role in resolving a bat-poop dispute that flared up between the U.S. and Peru in 1852. Businessmen mining those huge deposits of guano would have lost a fortune had Fillmore not stepped in.

Rabbits Worse Than Bats?

Although rabbits are fornicators of legendary capacity, what is not so well known is that like bats, they are also one of nature's very prolific defecators, dropping pellets at a rate of three every half minute while awake. That works out to more than 3,000 pellets per day per rabbit. But when it comes to production, rabbits pale in comparison to the blue whale, for whom about three tons a day is normal. (Even more impressive is the discovery in 2005 by researchers at the University of Manchester that your pillow collects up to two pounds of dust mite excrement per year no matter how often you wash your hair!)

They don't. Like most mammals, these leather-winged creatures of the order *Chiroptera* operate on the principle of "last thing before I go to sleep/first thing when I get up," which, if nothing else, makes clear that the least messy time to enter a bat cave may be in the dead of night.

9

Ducks quack—except for Muscovy ducks; they hiss. Elephants trumpet, monkeys chatter and bark, while sheep bleat and donkeys bray.

What do kangaroos do?

Do Crocodiles Shed Tears?

No. What happens is that a tear-like lubricant runs from their eyes to the jaws to help in swallowing prey. The tears fable was started by English writer Edward Topsell, in the 1500s. He also advised that the best way to scare off a crocodile is to stare at it with your right eye and wink at it with your left.

Cows moo? Says who?

We humans use imitative words for animal sounds, the vocabulary usually varying with the degree of affection (or lack of) we have for the beast in question. Despite their importance to our well being, for example, when it comes to cows we have only the rather pedestrian "moo," although for rare moments of bovine excitement there's "bawl," and for even rarer moments of romantic surge, we say "low." One school of thought attributes the meagerness of this cow-sound lexicon to our annoyance that a typical cow belches and farts about 106 pounds of methane per year into the atmosphere. On the other hand, any dog owner will readily admit the flatulent powers of your average *canis familiaris* are just as overwhelming, yet our words for their speech go far beyond bark and growl to include yip, yap, yaup, yelp, whine, whimper, howl, bell, and even in elevated moments, ululation. Doesn't seem fair.

They cluck. In a world where giraffes moan, weasels chirp, and oysters whistle, a clucking kangaroo should not raise any eyebrows, especially since these are natural sounds, not learned ones. Thus when you hear a raven cronk, you know it's not something he learned from watching championship tennis.

CATEGORY

6

Weirdness

1

“Gentlemen Prefer Blondes.”

Do they?

Barbers think outside the box?

Individual strands of hair don't grow at the same rate; about 10% of your head is at rest at any one time and it's the resulting differences in length that keep driving us to the salon or barbershop. That fact never seems to keep barbers busy enough, for they are notorious for operating other businesses on the side. Best example: in rural areas of the Republic of Yemen, as recently as the turn of the century you could still get a circumcision with your haircut. Not exactly on the side, but definitely outside the box.

Who's Got the Most Hair?

The survey didn't mention that blondes have the most hair, about 140,000 strands per average head as opposed to 105,000 for brunettes and 90,000 for redheads. (If you wonder who does the counting for stuff like this, never underestimate how frantically candidates in post-grad biology are looking for something to do.) Hair follicles replace themselves approximately every 56 days. That's on your head. Elsewhere on your body they last longer, although science has established that in the case of facial hair, blondes, whether or not they have more fun, definitely have more speed: blond facial hair grows the fastest of all. Which could well mean—although no one has yet done the research—that blondes are comparatively more subject to pognophobia (fear of beards).

Not according to Harlequin, the world's largest publisher of romance novels. In a survey of 1000 men, Harlequin discovered that 310 preferred brunettes, while 290 chose blondes. 180 men went for black hair, 90 picked redheads, and 30 gave the nod to gray. That left 100 who had no opinion or were smart enough to keep their mouths shut.

2

John Steinbeck plucked a phrase out of a line by Scottish poet Robbie Burns, and used it for the title of his Pulitzer Prize winner, *Of Mice and Men*. Burns used the line in "To a Mouse," written when he unearthed a cozy mouse nest with his plow. You know the line: "The best laid plans o' mice and men . . ."

What's the rest of the line?

And the Dean?

While the chronicle reports that the dean held on to his prayer book throughout the attempted copulation, there is no mention that he continued to pray.

What Went Wrong?

Talk about "gang aft agley!" A sensible plan on the surface, but the mare chosen for her docility and parade experience also happened to be in heat that day. While she herself was sufficiently well-trained to control her primal urges, the opportunity—perhaps heightened by the stimulating sight of Dean Price in solemn prayer—was too much for a young stallion stationed in the cathedral square. He threw his rider, mounted the mare and performed with unbridled enthusiasm, entirely uninhibited by the very public venue or by the struggles of the dean trapped beneath him.

". . . . often go wrong."

His actual words in Scottish dialect are "gang aft agley." Burns published the poem in 1785, so the warning came too late for a pompous English churchman, the Reverend Doctor Price, Dean of Hereford. To mark special holy days, it was customary for the dean to lead a procession through the streets of Hereford to the steps of the cathedral. In 1593, when the feast day of the cathedral's patron saint came round, the usual parade was organized with Doctor Price scheduled to walk at its head. That year however, the worthy dean opted to break with tradition. Rather than proceed afoot as the common clergy did, a position that put him at eye—and nose—level with the unwashed masses, he decided to ride a pretty white mare. From this comparatively lofty position, he reasoned, his flock would be more certain to see him offering inspiration because he would be reading a book of prayer en route.

3

Wearing a "Stetson" identifies you as a Westerner (or wishing you were). These large, wide-brimmed cowboy hats are called "ten-gallon hats" because they were once marketed to cowboys and travelers in the west as being able to carry water.

ONE UP

How much water does a ten-gallon hat hold?

Do Feathers Weigh More Than Gold?

Any trivia buff worth his salt knows that a pound of feathers outweighs a pound of gold. That's because medieval gold traders operated mostly out of Troyes in France, where merchants used a ratio of twelve ounces to the pound (hence troy weight). Elsewhere, merchants of bulkier stuff like coal and wool (and feathers) opted for sixteen ounces to the pound (avoirdupois weight). This could explain why globalization was not a problem in the sixteenth century.

Add to all the above the fact that the English horn comes from Vienna, that Panama hats don't come from Panama and that the Canary Islands are actually named for wild dogs, it's comforting to think that Grant is actually buried in Grant's Tomb—well, technically not buried; he's entombed there.

Is It Exactly Three-Qrarters?

For those who pursue accuracy, a Stetson holds three liters. The "about" in three quarts is a product of the impossibly messy imperial measuring system to which the U.S and England still cling. Although the rest of the world has gone metric, these two countries hang on to things like the "foot," a unit made up by Henry I in 1180 when he decreed that a foot would be one-third the length of his arm. (Not hard to figure how he came up with his decree for "yard.")

About three quarts. Ironically, John Batterson Stetson, who designed this emblem of the American west, was born and raised in New Jersey, and his factory opened in 1869 in Philadelphia. But then in a world where Chinese Checkers comes from Sweden, and camel hair brushes are made from squirrel fur, that's no surprise.

4

The voice says "press number sign" and you hit [#]. If you hear "ampersand" you press [&] and for "plus" it's [+]. Then there's [@], and [$], and [/], and [*], and . . . The keyboard is full of these symbols that take the place of words.

What are these things called?

Adding to your Pickup Lines?

If your target in a singles bar is not impressed when you open by pointing out that that the weird signs used to show swearing in comic books are jarns, nettles, grawlices, and quimps, then try these: The symbol for paragraph [¶] is called a pilcrow, and when your printer produces an imperfection, especially one caused by a wrinkle in the paper, that's called a mackle. If none of this works, try your luck with "tittle." That's the dot over the letter *i*.

Anybody for an octothorp?

Voice mail systems call the octothorp [#] the "pound" or "number sign," despite the fact that [#] is not a number sign until it precedes a number, as in Suite #211; it is not a pound sign until it follows a number, as in 40# keg of nails. An even bigger confusion surrounds the [@]. In every language that uses it [@] stands for "at." But in French, it's called a *commercial* or "commercial A." In Spain, Portugal, and Mexico, and in South and Central America it's called an *arroba*. In German it's an *affenschwanz* (monkey's tail), and in English it has no name at all.

Grammalogues. Or sometimes, logograms.

Curiously, despite universal agreement on what individual grammalogues mean, there is almost no agreement on their individual names. Take the virgule [/],for example, which substitutes for "per" as in parts/million and for "or" as in has/has not. (In the late twentieth century it also had a brief and ugly life as a gender-yoke as in s/he.) By the twenty-first century, however, for all but the most rigorously literate, computers had turned the virgule into "backslash."

5

Elephants, supposedly, are terrified of mice.

Are they really?

Or maybe These?

There is no word for the general's phobia, although some other truly weird fears have earned identities. *Helminthophobia*, for example, is the irrational fear of being infested with worms, and if you have *parthenophobia* you are afraid of virgins. Strangely, although there are words for the fear of dogs (*cynophobia*) and cats (*aelurophobia*) there is no phobia name for fear of kangaroos. Since fully one-third of all car accidents in Canberra, Australia are kangaroo-related it's probably time there was.

Any of these phobias yours?

Phobias are so interesting that it's often hard to separate the genuine ones that appear in the psychiatric literature (*ergasiophobia*—fear of work; *eosophobia*—fear of dawn), from the jokes (*friendorphobia*—fear of forgetting a password; *arachibyturiphobia*—fear of peanut butter sticking to the roof of your mouth). A common but very genuine number fear is *triskaidekaphobia*. One of its better known sufferers was Franklin Delano Roosevelt who would never sit at a table set for thirteen. Other genuine phobias, although rare, seem so wacko they're hard to believe. Case in point: Gebhard von Blücher, the Prussian general who showed up at the last minute to turn the tide against Napoleon at the Battle of Waterloo. General Blücher, his biographers insist, had a morbid fear that he was born with a womb and was carrying a yet-to-be-born animal in it!

Only in cartoons. Irrational fear of mice and rats is called *myophobia* and it's real, all right, but elephants don't have it. Like other ruminant quadrupeds though, they are prone to *sciaphobia* (easily spooked by shadows) which may explain why, every February, it's Punxatawny Phil who does the see-my-shadow schtick and not Jumbo.

6

The Miss America pageant is held every year in Atlantic City, New Jersey and has been since 1921. But it was not the world's first national contest of this type. That happened in Europe in 1888.

In what country?

On the up and up?

The idea for Barbie sprang from the brain of Jack Ryan (who, for trivia buffs, was the sixth of Zsa Zsa Gabor's nine husbands). The idea for the Atlantic City pageant came from newspaper reporter, Herb Test, who is also celebrated for making the contest as fair and honest as possible. Fairness was not exactly the case in the world's first dog show, held in Newcastle-on-Tyne, England, in 1859, open only to setters and pointers. The owner of the dog that won the pointer class was the judge for the setter class, and the guy who won the setter class judged the pointers. Nothing that sleazy has ever happened in Atlantic City.

A Record-Holding Miss America?

Margaret, who entered as Miss Washington D.C., owns four records that still stand. She is the first Miss America—that will stand forever—but she is also the youngest ever (just fifteen and still in high school), and so far is the shortest (five feet, one inch), and, to be politically correct, the least dimensional. Her vital stats were a deflating 30-25-32. By way of comparison, the measurements of Mattel Inc.'s Barbie, if she were human size, would pro-rate to 39-21-33.

No, not France but Belgium. The winner was an eighteen-year-old Creole girl from the island of Guadeloupe named Bertha Soucaret, and almost nothing is known about her because she was hidden from everyone except the judges! In Atlantic City's first pageant, things were a lot different: the winner, Margaret Gorman, and all her competitors were paraded publicly at every event.

7

The most common surname in the U.S. is Smith.

What's the second most common surname in the U.S.?

Is There a Chinese Version of Smith?

On a world-wide basis, the Smiths are mere piffle compared to the Changs (also written Chan) in China. The name attaches to about 11 per cent of the population of China, which means that in that country alone, the Changs outnumber the population of most countries in the world.

How Do All the Smiths Manage?

Since there are more than 100,000 *John* Smiths at any one time, some Smith parents attempt to distinguish their offspring by avoiding an ordinary first name at all costs. Among the more memorable forays in the U.S. registry are Kaboodle Smith, Suryat Smith, Everything Smith, and in a truly vigorous attempt at distinction, Smith Smith.

Some Smiths are quite content with their names, such as the brothers of cough drop fame. That's Andrew on the right of the box and William on the left. Blues singer Trixie Smith kept her name too, although she is better known among trivia buffs for recording "My Daddy Rocks Me with One Steady Roll" for Black Swan Records in 1922. It was one of the first times in recorded music that "rock and roll" was used as a metaphor for sex. Less content, however, was Gladys Smith, the real name of movie mega-star Mary Pickford who became "America's Sweetheart" even though she was from Canada. Then there's an entirely forgettable Smith: Emma, an Englishwoman who took aim at *The Guinness Book of Records* by having herself buried alive for 101 days.

Johnson, according to the U.S. Census Bureau.

Jones doesn't come in till number four. Williams is third and Brown rounds out the top five. In sixth is Davis, and completing the top ten in order are Miller, Wilson, Moore and Taylor.

8

Hold your arms straight out in front of you, parallel with the floor, palms up. Now focus on any point beyond the tips of your fingers. Keep your hands still.

On your shirt or blouse, which side has the buttons, right or left, and which side has the buttonholes?

Do Lefties Ever Get a Break?

Although lefties have trouble using scissors and playing the saxophone, and despite the fact that no leftie to date has won the world horseshoe pitching title, the news is not all bad. Writing Hebrew is easier for them and so is unscrewing jar tops. And lefties have a friend in the north: polar bears may have no use for jars, but they show a clear left paw preference in both defense and attack.

Do You Know These Lefties?

No one knows if Jack the Ripper needed help buttoning up, but Scotland Yard concluded he was left-handed. So was his contemporary, Queen Victoria, and she did have help. Neil Armstrong stepped onto the moon left foot first. Captain Ahab would have if he'd been there, but it was his left leg that was missing, as was Captain Hook's left hand and Vincent van Gogh's left ear.

For women, it's buttons on the left, for men it's on the right.

It has been that way for centuries in the clothing industry. Men—contemporary men—have the advantage if, like 89–90% of the world, they are right handed, for it's easier to push buttons on the right through holes on the left. The design for women comes from social history. When buttons came into popular use in the thirteenth century, replacing hooks, pins, and belts, only the wealthy could afford them. While men generally dressed themselves, wealthy ladies were dressed by their right-handed servants who faced their mistresses and buttoned away. Not many servants do this any more but the button placement has stuck.

9

Biographers of Sarah Bernhardt (1844-1923)—the actress, novelist, playwright, and recording star known as "The Divine Sarah"—claim that for sixty years, not a single day passed without mention of her in a newspaper somewhere around the world. Yet at the very peak of her career, in her own native France, when it came to filling concert halls she was never able to outdraw a wildly popular performer named Joseph Pujol.

What did Pujol do on stage that made him such a fantastic hit?

Whose taste? Whose etiquette?

Unlike Sarah Bernhardt—who became rich and famous using Madonna-like behavior to attract attention—like sleeping in a coffin lined with letters from her lovers—Joseph Pujol became rich and famous while being very restrained. His audiences, however, regularly went nuts, becoming so enervated by laughter that the Moulin Rouge kept a staff of nurses in the aisles to treat mass fainting. Which says something about the true regard for this etiquette-laden bodily function.

Unlimited whiffs of talent?

Having trained his innards to take in and retain air, Pujol could last for an hour and a half on stage. He offered an incredible range of flatulent entertainments, like imitating popular opera stars, presenting night scenes with hooting owls and amorous bullfrogs, or pretending to be an artilleryman commanding several types of cannon fire. One of his most popular routines by far was the bride's fart on the wedding night and then a comparison after a year of marriage. Pujol would have the audience close their eyes and then challenge them to distinguish between a blast from a trumpet and his imitation. He would blow out candles from a variety of distances and offer the tonic scale (key of B major) with pitch-pipe accuracy. A regular feature was his encore: he would have the audience stand while he pumped out the first line of the French national anthem.

He farted. Under the stage name "Le Petomane" (the farter), Pujol became the toast of Europe and continued to be a leading act at the Moulin Rouge from 1892 until he retired his talented derrière in 1914.

CATEGORY 7

History

1

"Damn the torpedoes! Full speed ahead!" That was Admiral Farragutt, leading an attack on Confederate positions in Mobile Bay, Alabama, in 1864. But torpedoes as we know them weren't invented until after the Civil War.

So what was Farragutt damning?

What was Farragutt saying?

Farragutt actually said, "Full speed ahead, Drayton!" The admiral was lashed to the rigging for a better view of the battle, and when a "torpedo" (what we'd call a mine today) sank one of his ships and threw the fleet into confusion, he ordered his flag captain (Drayton) to barrel on through. It worked.

How Reliable Are Torpedoes?

For the next century, torpedoes boasted only a so-so reliability. Take, for example, the Allied attack on the massive German battleship, *Bismarck*, on May 26, 1941, in the north Atlantic. Ten torpedo planes swooped down on *Bismarck*, directed in by the British cruiser, *Sheffield*, but all ten torpedoes either exploded on hitting the water or immediately took dead aim for the bottom of the sea. All for the best, as it turned out, for the planes had targeted the *Sheffield!* This was similar to the misdirected effort of a British bomber just two days into the war. After spotting a submarine on the surface along the coast of Scotland, the bomber dove in low and dropped a pair of 100-lb. bombs on it, both of which missed and bounced back up to explode on either side of the plane. Since the submarine happened to be a British one, the crew declined to help with the rescue of the bomber crew.

Floating beer kegs filled with gunpowder.

The motorized torpedo wasn't invented until 1870 by an Englishman. In 1878, a Russian warship launched a torpedo in the Black Sea and gave Turkey the dubious honor of becoming the first country to lose a ship to one. Eight years later (1886) the Greek navy announced it had the world's first torpedo-armed submarine (made in Sweden).

2

Spanish explorer, adventurer, and all round nogoodnik Vasco de Balboa was the first non-native person to cross North America from the Atlantic to the Pacific.

Who was first to go *around* North America?

Did they have help?

Mackenzie, as well as Lewis and Clark, acknowledged that they'd likely never have made it without the help of native peoples along the way. Not Balboa, who went out of his way to exterminate as many as he could. More peaceful by far, if less dramatic, was the help given Englishman Vivian Fuchs, in the first crossing of Antartica in 1958. He had two secret weapons: one was his second-in-command, Sir Edmund Hillary (the Mount Everest Hillary); the other was machinery. On Hillary's advice, Fuchs used farm tractors to cross the frozen continent.

What about Lewis and Clark?

They come in third in the crossing-the-continent record book. A decade or so before their trip, William Mackenzie crossed Canada from the Atlantic to the Pacific and then went up to the Arctic, thereby becoming number two to cross. Mackenzie wrote a book about his adventures entitled *Voyages from Montreal through the Continent of North America*. The book intrigued President Thomas Jefferson, who then turned to his private secretary, Meriwether Lewis, and said, "I've got an idea for an interesting trip."

Scientists and crew on the *CSS Hudson*, a Canadian government research vessel. In November, 1969, the Hudson headed south from Halifax, Nova Scotia, down the Atlantic coast, and after rounding South America, crossed the Pacific lengthwise, traversed the Bering Sea, then sailed through the Northwest Passage and down the north Atlantic coast, returning to Halifax in November, 1970. Along the way they did an in-depth study of the fjords of Chile, which may explain why there's never been a Hollywood movie about this trip.

3

Two women figured prominently in the siege of Troy. One is the legendary beauty known as Helen of Troy. But you knew that.

Who is the other one?

Does Science Make a Difference?

In today's world, it's much easier to believe pronouncements made by those in authority. Take the announcement by the World Health Organization in Geneva, on May 16, 1975, informing the world that "malaria has been licked." On that very day the deputy director of WHO, Dr. Thomas Lambo, was rushed to hospital.

With malaria.

Ups and Downs in the Prediction Business?

The Trojan story doesn't tell us whether Cassandra ever said "I told you so," but in the year 1348, the medical faculty at the University of Paris sure did. In April of that year, this august group, applying the medical science of the time, issued a bulletin saying that Saturn, Jupiter, and Mars had all shown up together in the House of Aquarius for the first time in decades, so a calamity was imminent. Like most medical advice it was ignored, and two months later, the Black Death arrived in France.

A more recent example arose on the morning of December 6, 1941, when Secretary of the Navy, Frank Knox, asked the War Plans Department of the U.S. Navy if Japan might attack. "No," he was assured by Admiral Turner, "they're not ready for us yet."

Cassandra, the sister of Paris, the guy who started the whole affair by getting Helen to run off with him.

Cassandra's is a good news/bad news story, for she had the bad luck to stir the hormones of the god Apollo. Instead of wine and roses, Apollo wooed her by giving her the ability to predict the future, but when Cassandra told him "Not tonight! In fact, not ever!" Apollo fixed it so that no one would ever believe her predictions. Thus, when Cassandra told the Trojans that the big wooden horse the Greeks left behind was going to be big trouble, no one paid attention.

4

If you were paying attention in the seventh grade, you know the Hundred Years War between England and France did not really go on for a hundred years.

So how long was the Hundred Years War?

The Shortest War?

Nations, if they must fight, should consider the titanic struggle of Sultan Sa'îd Khalid of Zanzibar who declared war on the British Empire on August 27, 1896. From declaration to surrender the entire war lasted thirty-seven minutes. And this war doesn't have a name.

What to call a war?

The War of Jenkin's Ear (1739-48) was really about who would get the throne of Austria, even though Captain Robert Jenkins sailed all the way home to England from the Caribbean with his ear in a jar just to prove the Spanish were bad guys. Then there's the War of the Spanish Succession (1701-13) which was really between France and England, and the War of the Triple Alliance (1864-70). In this one, Brazil, Argentina, and Uruguay almost wiped out Paraguay, reducing its population from one and a half million to two hundred thousand in just six years, which may be why Paraguay gets no mention in the name of the war.

One hundred and sixteen years, from 1337 to 1453.

Fighting was sporadic though, because both sides were always taking time off to look after matters at home. Even the actual battles were often interrupted by things like bad weather. Armored knights were highly conscious of rust so neither side wanted to fight in the rain. A battle would usually be put on hold over Sundays or feast days, and if the leader of one side was ill or indisposed, it was not uncommon for the other to offer a halt out of courtesy. Thus, by these standards, a better choice for a really long war is the struggle between Spain and the Moors of North Africa, which began in 718 and lasted until 1492, the year Columbus landed in America.

5

Think ancient Egypt. Ptolemy IV has called a meeting, but the high priest is late. Could it be he forgot to go outside to check the time? Why outside? Because the Egyptians (and other ancient cultures) used sundials.

How did they tell time at night?

Why pay retail?

The world's most expensive watch (so far) is the Graves "33," a wristwatch made in 1933 for U.S. millionaire Henry Graves, which tells the time and date, and shows graphic displays of sun and moon phases. It took over three years to make. In 2004, instead of going to the Museum of Time as planned, the Graves "33" was sold to a private collector for just over eleven million dollars. In 2005 a knockoff became available by mail order for under a hundred bucks.

When Did Watches Appear?

Mainsprings were invented in Germany around 1500, making watches possible. They quickly became a status symbol, but early ones were so bulky the typical owner had his carried by a servant. Minute hands appeared in England (1670) but wristwatches did not show up until the 1790s, in Switzerland. The self-winding watch was patented in 1924 and the first waterproof model, a Rolex, in 1926. The first alarm watch was patented in France right after World War II. By this time, the Bulova Watch Company was so successful that even though it had developed the quartz crystal system in the 1920s, it was not introduced in retail until the 1970s.

With water clocks, similar in operation to sandglasses.

The first mechanical timepiece on record (China in 1088) used water, too, but for power. Europe's first clock (1283) used weights. It was built at a monastery, one of the few institutions of the period for which accurate time was important because of the rigidly timed schedule of prayers laid down by Saint Benedict. (The new mechanical clock must have delighted the monk in charge of waking up the others, because it had been customary for him to sleep with a precisely measured—and lit—candle between his toes!)

6

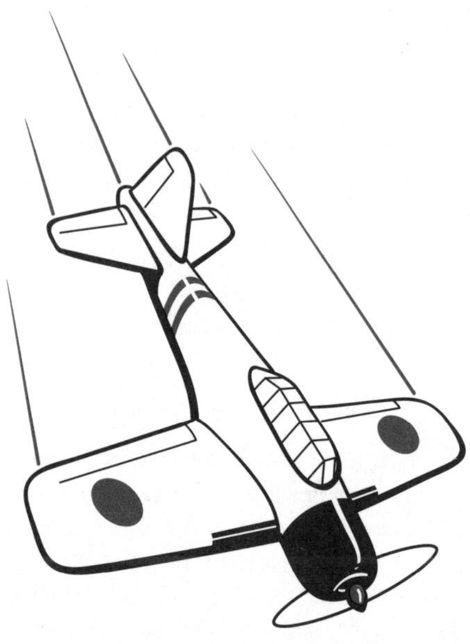

By the middle of 1945, every U.S. sailor—indeed everybody in the world—knew about "kamikaze" pilots.

What does "kamikaze" mean?

Just like the CIA?

The Mongols, like the CIA, had a reputation for trying out any kind of new weapon no matter how absurd it seemed. The U.S. Army may have been following their example in 1943 when it authorized an experiment in which small flash bombs were attached to live bats, the intent being to release hordes of them over German cities at night. According to declassified documents the army had thousands of bats ready to go by 1945, but the experiment was abandoned when a large colony escaped and destroyed an aircraft hangar.

Perhaps they were undertrained.

"Divine wind."

In the year 1274 and again in 1281, Asia's dreaded Mongol invaders sent a fleet to conquer Japan and both times a freak windstorm blew it out of the water. Although the virtually unstoppable Mongols had conquered China, Russia, much of the Middle East, and huge hunks of Europe, Japan was one of their rare failures (along with Burma where the Mongolian cavalry was spooked by regiments of elephants).

Considerably less successful in dealing with the Mongols was Pope Innocent IV. Perhaps because he had neither elephants nor kamikazes readily available, he sent a sixty-year old Franciscan friar, Giovanni Carpini, deep into Asia with an offer of baptism if the Mongols stopped their invasions. The guffaws from Guyuk Khan, grandson of the mighty Genghis, surprised no one except Innocent—and maybe the friar—so just about all this pointless mission accomplished was to make Carpini the first European to cross Asia (beating Marco Polo by almost three decades).

7

In 1775 the Continental Congress set up the postal system and appointed Ben Franklin as Postmaster General.

When did the U.S. government start issuing stamps?

Whose Idea Was This?

South Africa had the first triangular stamps, while China still owns the biggest ever—about 2-1/2" x 8". Tiny Bhutan, high in the Himalayas, issued a stamp in 1973 in the shape of a record. On one side was a recording of the Bhutanese national anthem in 45 rpm.

When did We Stop Licking?

The first woman ever to appear on a stamp was Queen Victoria. It was also the world's first adhesive stamp, and that caused a fuss among the upper classes who felt it was wrong to be licking the royal backside. The first country to issue self-adhesive stamps was Sierra Leone, which may or not have led to an obesity academic in that African country, because licking a stamp uses up about ⅒th of a calorie.

Not until 1847.

This was 22 years after it set up a national dead letter department. (First things first.) The premier issue was a red-brown five-cent depicting Franklin and a ten-cent black with the image of George Washington. Since then, Washington has appeared on stamps more often than any other person. (The first woman on a U.S. stamp was not Martha Washington, but Queen Isabella of Spain). Initially, stamps were pretty much limited to the faces of presidents (like the 2¢ "Black Jack" of Andrew Jackson, first issued in 1863), but it didn't take long to branch out. Today there are stamps with images as diverse as Sitting Bull, Knute Rockne, and John Philips Sousa, not to mention historical events (moon landing) transportation (especially trains) and native animals (camels have shown up twice).

8

Thanks to Shakespeare, who messed around with history quite freely, Macbeth has a bad rep, so when Macduff kills him at the end of the play, the audience is quite satisfied. The fact is the real Macbeth wasn't a bad king at all. And it wasn't the real Macduff who killed him, either.

So who did?

A Day to Remember?

Macbeth, according to the Holinshed Chronicles, met his end on August 15, an auspicious day for comings and goings in history. It's the birthday of modern India in 1947, for example, and of South Korea, and it's also the day in 1769 when Maria Bonaparte gave birth to a little boy in Corsica whom she named Napoleon.

August 15 is the birthday (in 1860) of Florence Kling who, when she married, became Florence Kling DeWolfe, and then a few years later, Florence Kling DeWolfe Harding, after she dumped her first husband to marry the man who would become twenty-ninth president of the United States. Among other things, this powerful woman (often called "Mrs. President" by White House staff) is alleged to have entered the Oval Office one day without knocking, much to the annoyance of the commander-in-chief, who was busily engaged on top of his desk—and a secretary. Fortunately, August 15 also harbors a moral counterpoint to this event, because it is a day the Vatican has picked to celebrate the Virgin Mary.

Also on August 15: Guy Zinn of the Yankees stole home twice in the same game. That was in 1912.

Malcolm. He, too, was in the play and like the others, he's real.

In the year 1057, Malcolm not only took out Macbeth but also Macbeth's son, Lulach. Aficionados of Shakespeare are quick to note that although Lulach was real, he does not appear in the play. Either Shakespeare didn't know what to do with him, or it could be that perhaps he really did. To his contemporaries (and mostly behind his back) Macbeth's son was known as Lulach the Fatuous. Apparently he was not a candidate for the gifted class.

9

On June 1, 1813, the *USS Chesapeake* was going head to head with a British ship off Boston harbor when the fatally wounded captain of the U.S. ship gave his last command to the crew: the immortal cry of "Don't give up the ship!"

Did the crew follow orders?

More "Truman Truth" needed?

Over time, public figures have become wary of media that twist their words and a public that loves to swallow them. That may explain why one of America's most no-nonsense presidents was so crystal-clear when he fired a most accomplished "spinner," General Douglas MacArthur. "I didn't fire him because he was a dumb son of a bitch," Harry Truman explained, "although he was. But [being dumb] is not against the law for generals. If it was, half to three-quarters of them would be in jail."

Putting a Spin on History?

No subject seems more susceptible to phony spin than military history. Teddy Roosevelt's Rough Riders, for example, didn't "charge" up San Juan Hill in Cuba; they walked because they had no horses. In any case it was Kettle Hill, not San Juan, and an African-American unit did most of the fighting. Then there's "Don't fire until you see the whites of their eyes!" credited in American mythology to William Prescott at the Battle of Bunker Hill in 1775 (really fought on Breed's Hill). But Prescott was simply plagarizing Frederick the Great, who used it decades before. In the Civil War, General Sherman's "Hold the Fort!" is a spin, because what he actually signaled was "Hold out: relief is coming!" Sherman gets credit, too, for "War is hell!" but always insisted that he never said it. He did say, however, that newspaper reporters are "dirty scribblers with the impudence of Satan," so it's easy to understand who might have made up the story.

No. They surrendered and the *Chesapeake* was towed away. Her captain's final words are now part of American myth, but losing the battle is conveniently forgotten.

CATEGORY

8

The Arts

1

If James Whistler is one of America's best-known painters, then Whistler's mother, in her rocking chair, is one of the country's best-known models.

What's the title of this famous painting?

Expanding his Horizons?

When poor health and old age brought on a decline in Anna's monitoring, Whistler happily returned to his old habits, fathering two more children and taking on eccentricities somewhat weird even for the Left Bank, like wearing red pumps with pink bows. He also went bankrupt. To the end, Whistler scoffed at art lovers who admired the portrait of his mother, but he must have picked up some of her traits, for he began to sue critics over bad reviews. He also became an author. *The Gentle Art of Making Enemies* was published in 1890.

How Did Mom do It?

After being kicked out of West Point, Whistler went to Paris to study painting, using a hefty inheritance to support himself. But he never went to his lessons, concentrating instead on developing a modest string of illegitimate children. After nearly ten years of this he seemed to be settling down with his favorite mistress/model, Joanne Hiffernan who, conveniently, happened to be both drop-dead gorgeous and easy to get along with. At this point, however, Anna took a ship to Paris, got rid of Joanne, and moved in to monitor her son full-time. The new arrangement dramatically slowed Whistler's production—of both paintings and children—but also tended to discourage his models. When one failed to show on a day in 1871, it was decided that Anna would take on her role, a step that clearly called for clothing and, at the last moment, a rocking chair.

"Arrangement in Gray and Black No. 1."

Although it's widely known as "Whistler's Mother," that title implies a degree of affection the artist did not feel. Whistler found Mom (Anna) pretty hard to take. So did just about everybody else. Not all her fault, however, for it took a lot of parent power to manage James Abbott Whistler.

2

The world's most-quoted book is the Bible. No argument there. And coming in an easy number two is Shakespeare's works.

What comes in third?

What Happened?

Unlike Walt Whitman's *Leaves of Grass* or the incredibly pornographic *Fanny Hill* (America's first obscenity case), Alice got into Boston okay. So did Martin Luther's writings even though they were banned by the Vatican. Twice too, once in 1521 and again in 1930 for good measure. The Vatican also banned James Joyce's *Ulysses*, (which suggests someone there actually read it; no mean task). *Ulysses* has even been burned in public—which puts it in good literary company. *Brave New World, Huck Finn*, and *To Kill a Mockingbird*, have all felt flame. *Catcher in the Rye* still suffers even in the twenty-first century, and has been joined by the *Harry Potter* books. But not Alice. Even though Lewis Caroll, an unmarried oddball, often exhibited behaviors that would make today's parents call the cops if he came near!

Except in China

Alice was banned in China because animals in the story talked like humans. Curiously, however, the censors there had no problem with the Mad Hatter, possibly because they had some sympathy for him. Traditionally, to stabilize woolen materials, hat makers used mercury, which they got by heating the mineral cinnabar. Anyone breathing the fumes from heated cinnabar becomes incredibly grouchy over time and will frequently descend into outright madness. In China, a lot of cinnabar was always being heated in backyards and little shops to make all those red banners of which Chairman Mao was so fond. (It might even explain his foreign policy.)

Alice's Adventures Under Ground or as it is better—albeit incorrectly—known, *Alice in Wonderland*.

According to the Smithsonian, the story that Lewis Carroll (real name: Charles Lutwidge Dodgson) first told to ten-year old Alice Liddell during a boating trip and then turned into a book, has never sagged in popularity since its surprise success at publication in 1865.

3

"*Did I get that wrong or what?*" Nothing is riskier than predicting the future of a piece of music or a musical style. A good example is the critic at the *New York Tribune* who called Gershwin's *Porgy and Bess* "sure-fire rubbish" on opening night. That's mild, however, compared to this description of rock'n'roll by an American musical giant. "It's phony and false," he declared, "written and played for the most part by cretinous goons."

Who said that?

“Dewey Defeats Truman?”

Not musical, but no goof list is complete without this legendary headline from the *Chicago Tribune*. Less well known, is the *Lancashire Evening Post* headline when news of the sinking of the *Titanic* first hit England. “All the Passengers Are Safe,” it declared. Honorable mention also goes to *Newsweek* in the early 1960s with “For the tourist who wants to get away from it all, try Vietnam,” and to the *Pacific Rural News* around the same time for “Sterility May Be Inherited.”

What is it about music?

Evangelist Billy Graham, no shrinking violet when it comes to making pronouncements, has been there too. He once made a big deal of breaking a personal rule—watching TV on a Sunday—in order to check out the Beatles when they performed on *The Ed Sullivan Show*, and immediately declared them a passing fad. Billy Graham was in good company, of course, for by that time the executive branch of Decca Records had rejected the Beatles because in their opinion “guitars are on the way out.” (Columbia and HMV turned down the Beatles, too.)

Ranking just as high on the goof scale in the early days of rock and roll were the producers of America’s most widely syndicated radio show for new talent, “Arthur Godfrey’s Talent Scouts.” When a group called the Blue Moon Boys auditioned in 1955, the producers said no way, in part because they didn’t like the way the lead singer performed. Over the next six years, this lead singer—Presley, of course—lobbed twenty-nine new releases in a row onto Billboard’s “Top Ten.” The thirtieth new song, released in 1963, only made it to number eleven. By this time, “Talent Scouts” was off the air.

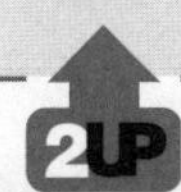

Frank Sinatra. He was reacting to praise for Elvis Presley. That was in 1957. A few years later he paid Presley a fortune to sing for just six minutes on a TV special.

Hard to prove, but this claim is probably true: in any one day in America, "Happy Birthday" is sung more often than the national anthem. Now, anybody can tell you that Francis Scott Key wrote the national anthem (okay, the lyrics).

Who wrote "Happy Birthday"?

Just how often?

On average, just over seventeen and a half million people a day are celebrating a birthday on our planet, and if only a fraction sang "Happy Birthday" and paid royalties, the income would challenge Bill Gates for supremacy. However, the copyright laws have an escape clause known as "one time personal use," so it's legal to sing it at home. That's good news for parents who might try to emulate former Polish king Augustus the Strong. He sired over three hundred children. (They would not have expected birthday parties anyway, because all but a few were illegitimate.) Augustus ruled Poland (and Saxony) from 1697 to 1706, and then again from 1710 to 1733. Seems he needed four years off to rest.

Singing "Happy Birthday" in your jail cell?

In 1924, "Good Morning to All" was published without permission in a songbook edited by Robert Coleman, who altered the lyrics of the second verse to "Happy birthday to you." Then when the song showed up ten years later in Irving Berlin's "As Thousands Cheer," a third Hill sister, Jessica, took the matter to court and won. People were flabbergasted to learn the song was not public property, not in the least Western Union, which promptly dropped it as a singing telegram. A few years later on Broadway, the great Helen Hayes was reduced to speaking it in the play, "Happy Birthday," so the producers could avoid paying royalties.

Mildred and Patty Hill. The two sisters were teachers at an experimental kindergarten in Kentucky and wrote the song to be used as a daily welcome song. It was published under copyright in 1893 with the title "Good Morning to All."

5

"Washington Crossing the Delaware" was painted by Emmanuel Leutze. The famous portrait has Washington standing up in an overcrowded boat in bad weather: irresponsible behavior, and not at all typical of the first president. He's not crossing the Delaware, either, in this painting.

What river is it?

Other Crucial Details?

"Washington Crossing the Delaware" has hung in the Metropolitan Museum of Art in New York for over a century, but it's a replica. The original was destroyed by an Allied bomb in 1943. As for Walter Johnson, at the time of the media stunt and for years after, he held the major league record for most wild pitches.

Big League Baseball Supports the President?

With the exception of quips and sayings attributed to Lincoln and inventions said to be Ben Franklin's, no American figure is surrounded by more fables than George Washington, but one actually has a grain of truth: his alleged throwing of a coin across the Potomac. According to the first president's cousins, he had developed the idle habit of throwing not coins but *stones* across the river. (Throwing coins would have been as much out of character as standing up in a boat.) Also according to the cousins, the river was actually another Virginia stream, the Rappahannock. A media setup in 1936, organized to test the truth of the coin story, employed yet another legend, big league fastballer Walter "Big Train" Johnson. With cameras whirring while he did his windup at about the point where Washington would have—if indeed he did—Johnson heaved a silver dollar across the Rappahannock with distance to spare, thereby confirming that the story could be true.

The Rhine. There were many images of Washington around to guide Leutze by the time he started the painting (1850), but for realism he needed a river to model. Since his studio was in Dusseldorf, the Rhine was a lot closer than the Delaware. Leutze didn't stop there, either. The boat is a different type and size than the one Washington used that Christmas Day in 1776, and although the stars and stripes fly prominently in the painting, the flag was not yet part of the campaign.

6

Many people call Beethoven's ninth symphony "Ode to Joy," because the composer set a favorite poem, "Ode to Joy," to music in the final movement. It is the only one of Ludwig van Beethoven's symphonies with a choral component, and one of the few symphonies by any composer that has one.

Who wrote "Ode to Joy"?

Beethoven Redux?

On Good Friday, 1988, during a performance of Beethoven's "Missa Solemnis" by the Ealing Choral Society, the entrance door of the hall banged open, and a figure in helmet, boots, and chains clanked up the aisle, terrifying audience, performers, and conductor alike. It turned out a college student with a part-time job delivering kiss-o-grams had blundered into the wrong hall. With the mix-up sorted out, he clumped back out; the conductor took up the baton and the music resumed. All present agreed the experience was a personal first. Likely for Beethoven, too.

Would You Invite Beethoven to Diner?

Beethoven never ran out on his sponsors, but if upset could be even more dramatic, one of the more notable examples being the time he tried to beat up his primary money source, Prince Lichnowsky, with a chair. To be fair, Beethoven didn't discriminate. He beat up on servants, waiters, his family, his publisher, and any musician that hit a wrong note. Even cows. (Local farmers at Gneixendorf, where his beautiful Pastoral Symphony was born, complained to authorities that Beethoven made their cattle run away.) He must have been a prize, too, as a dinner guest, for he had a habit of hawking and spitting at will.

Friedrich von Schiller (1759-1805) a high-profile contemporary of Beethoven who, if he'd knuckled under to his boss early on, would have gone on to be a nobody.

Schiller was a surgeon in the regiment of the Duke of Wurttemburg, but being more interested in writing than medicine or the military, he went AWOL one night to see the opening of his first play. The Duke confined him to barracks and, in a display of true Beethoven-like behavior, Schiller told the duke to stuff it and ran away, spending the next ten years writing and becoming famous throughout Europe.

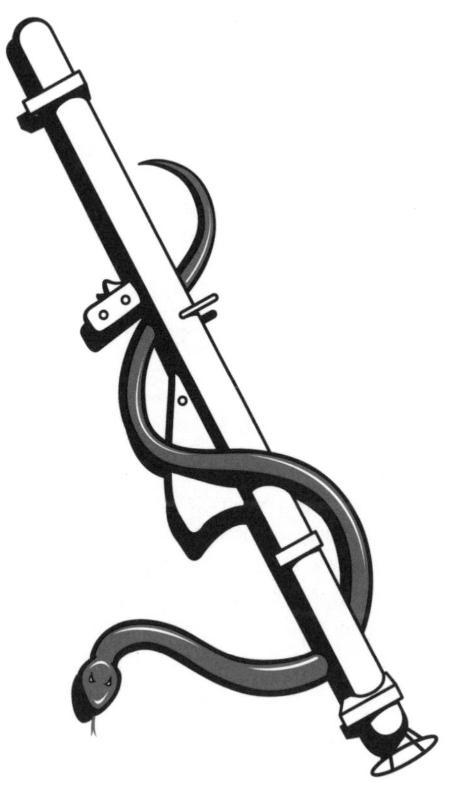

Bazooka. You know what that is. Serpent. You know that, too.

What do a bazooka and a serpent have in common with a hecklephone?

And Bazooka bubblegum?

Dubble Bubble pretty well controlled the chew-and-blow market until Bazooka Bubblegum made a challenge with marketing ploys like the World Series of Bubblegum Blowing. In 1975, Kurt Bevacqua of the Milwaukee Brewers took the title by sustaining an eighteen-inch globoid for twelve seconds. He won a year's supply of gum.

What About the Bazooka?

It's a crude mishmash of pipes invented by comedian Bob Burns in the 1920s and the military weapon is named after it! The hecklephone is a double reed, baritone oboe invented by Wilhelm Heckel. Paul Whitman used one in his famous Aeolian Hall concert in 1924 (at which Gershwin's "Rhapsody in Blue" premiered), while the serpent is a bass cornet developed almost five centuries ago. Mendelssohn, Berlioz, and Rossini used a serpent in their works but it's a museum piece now, having been replaced around 1850 by the ophicleide—which in turn fell before the bass tuba.

They are all musical instruments.

So is a "jouhikko." It has three horsehair strings over a sound box that rests on the performer's thigh and is bowed like a violin, while the other hand lifts the strings instead of pressing down on frets. The jouhikko took about 900 years to pretty much disappear since its first recorded use, but was revived for the musical version of *The Lord of the Rings* in 2006. Musicians who can actually play the thing are as rare as the instrument itself, but all describe the sound as "very liquid."

8

Despite the fact that one of the parts is missing, Lisa Gherardini's face (better known as the "Mona Lisa") is quite possibly the most recognized visage in the world.

What's missing on the Mona Lisa face?

An Artesian Well of Inspiration?

In addition to the 1950s chart-topping single by Nat "King" Cole, musicians as diverse as Bob Dylan, Elton John and Willy Nelson have sung about Mona Lisa. Even Britney Spears has gotten into the act. Lisa has been on TV (*Star Trek: The Next Generation*) and every other medium, most notably perhaps, in *The Da Vinci Code*, both the novel and the movie. The estimated value of Mona Lisa changes with the times ($620 million in 2005). Only select works by Picasso come close. One wonders what he would think of that, because at the time of her disappearance in 1911, Picasso was brought in for questioning but was released on lack of evidence.

Does Mosa Lisa Travel?

Although completed in Italy, for most of its life "Mona Lisa" has been in France. Exceptions are a trip to New York and Washington in the early 1960s and ten years later to Tokyo and Moscow. These were official. An unofficial journey took place from 1911 to 1913, compliments of Vincenzo Perugia, an Italian carpenter who walked out of the Louvre with the "Mona Lisa" under his coat. During this absence, scammers made six "authenticated" sales of the painting to private collectors in the U.S. alone. Stolen art detectives could not have been well-trained at that time, because Mona was frequently on display in Italy during this time.

Eyebrows. Some aficionados argue that over time they were rubbed off during cleanings but that doesn't explain why the wispy curls on her shoulders are still intact. There's a hint of them present, so most likely Leonardo da Vinci—and Lisa—were being true to the eyebrow plucking fashion that prevailed in Florence at the time.

9

Irving Berlin wrote songs to cover every celebration imaginable, a list that inevitably begins with "White Christmas" and "Easter Parade."

What song did he write for Thanksgiving?

And the *Mayflower?*

The *Mayflower's* round trip to America was a final one. On return to England the ship was taken apart and the wood was used to build a pig barn.

Where Did Thanksgiving Really Start?

Far shakier in the Thanksgiving category is the legend that the pilgrims of New England were first off the mark with this celebration. In fact, they lagged Samuel Champlain and the early colonists in what is now the Canadian province of Nova Scotia by a good twenty years. In the autumn of 1605, Champlain established L'Ordre de Bon Temps (The Society of Good Cheer) to give thanks for blessings and good fortune. The society served wine, for which it built North America's first wine cellar (recently discovered at Port Royal, NS), established a fish farm to provide a source for chaudière (chowder), and adapted a bean and corn recipe from the Mic Mac native people to make succotash. And to ensure thanks was rendered gourmet-style, the society regularly sent an expedition to Cape Cod Bay for oysters. The real first Thanksgiving had class, although the thanks-givers may have been a bit heavy on the booze, for according to Champlain's meticulous records, consumption worked out to 250 bottles a member! Still, the winter of 1605 was a ferocious one, so if the colonists were able to get through it with a mild buzz, maybe they had much for which to be thankful.

"I Have so Much to Be Thankful for."

Odds are you've never heard it, but then odds are you haven't heard "Yiddle on Your Fiddle," either, or "Say It's Spinach" or "It Gets Lonely in the White House." But give the man a break. For someone who wrote over 1500 songs using only the black keys on the piano because he never learned to read music properly, Irving Berlin didn't do too badly. So if his Thanksgiving song was a bit of a dud, he has others in the repertoire to make up for it.

CATEGORY

9

Industry and Invention

CNN is on your TV screen. MVP is in the sports pages, and for MSN or IBM you turn to your computer. Those letter combinations are everywhere today. So is YKK.

Where do you look for YKK?

What's in a name?

Then along came B.F. Goodrich. Yes, the rubber guy. Although the new invention had pretty much fizzled (customers found them so hard to operate that each one was sold with a book of instructions!) Goodrich liked the idea. He especially liked the "zip" sound and is reputed to be the one who decreed that zippers should be called "zippers." In 1921 he ordered 170,000 for a new line of galoshes, and the rest, as they say. . . . By 1922 zippers were being sold without an instruction booklet.

Ever Use a "Clasplocker"?

Whitcomb Judson was an engineer from Chicago who was first to patent a zipper in 1893. He called it a "clasplocker" and since he already had a reputation as an inventor (e.g., brakes on railway cars), he took his new fastener to the Chicago World's Fair that year, expecting wide applause from the twenty-one million people who paid admission. The reaction was a big yawn. Judson sold a few to be used on mailbags, but there were no more orders—because they didn't really work. Twenty years later, another inventor, Gideon Sunbach, improved the design, called it the "slide fastener," and sold a big order to the military, but zippers still didn't catch on.

At the end of your zippers.

The average American buys twelve zippers a year, almost all of them made by a Japanese company founded by Yoshida Kogyo Kabushililaisha. YKK has over 200 manufacturing plants in 52 countries, with the one in Macon, GA, for example, producing over 1200 miles of zipper a day.

2

At the Indoor Plumbing Hall of Fame, if there were such a place, statues of Sir John Harrington, Alexander Cumming, and Thomas Crapper would have places of honor for their contribution to the convenience of flushing.

What did they invent?

Do Some Things Work Only at Home?

In 1852, a public lavatory was installed in London (one of the sponsors was Henry Cole, the father of the Christmas card). Despite heavy advertising, a pleasing name—Public Waiting Room—and spanking cleanliness, the new facility was a total bust, because Londoners simply refused to unbutton in public. After attracting just 58 flushes a month in the world's biggest city, it was shut down.

So who were these guys?

Harrington's model (1596) is often cited as the first, and although that's not true, the story of how it came about is interesting. He had run afoul of his godmother, Elizabeth I, for selling dirty books, and to regain favor presented a mechanical device at court for use in the royal loo. It flushed well and Her Majesty was duly impressed and ready to forgive, but Harrington got in trouble again, this time by publishing a joke book about the queen's new thunder box. He and the toilet were summarily deep-sixed, and interest in plumbing was thereby shut down until 1775, when Alexander Cumming lifted the lid once more. A flaw in Harrington's royal toilet was that it allowed odor to drift back up. To deal with this drawback, Cumming invented the "S" trap (S for "stink"), which is still used today. Nevertheless, another century passed before interest in flushing became popular, and that was largely because of Thomas Crapper, a businessman with flair. Using marketing ideas like aromatic toilet seats and surefire slogans like "Certain Flush with Easy Pull," he put flush toilets in the public eye so effectively that many today think of him as the inventor. (It helped that his name was stamped on every seat, too.)

Not the flush toilet. Flushing goes back to the Minoan civilization, 4000 years ago (and their kids always forgot. too!)

3

Levi Strauss was not the only tailor making pants for miners during the California gold rush, but his product was such a hit that it outsold the competition by a huge margin.

What was so special about the pants made by Levi Strauss?

Over-riveting?

Rivets helped make Strauss's fortune but they could have been a disaster. One crucial rivet location—at least in theory—is at the crotch where two vital seams cross, and Levi put one there. But not for long. Miners spend a lot of time squatting and when they did that in direct sunlight or at a campfire, the rivet heated up. Fortunately for Levi, he happened to join a group of miners around a campfire one night in time to witness a hot crotch dance first hand. The offending rivet was soon removed from the design.

How Did Levi Get the Inside Track?

Rivets were not his only sharp move. Levi was a shrewd observer of market demands. Although he first went to San Francisco to sell tents made from cotton canvas imported from Genoa (a city which French weavers pronounced "jeans"), he immediately switched to making "waist overalls" instead. His next move was to drop the Genoese cotton in favor of a more pliant twill from France called *serge de Nimes* ("denim"), to which he added yet another clever step. The new cloth was grayish-white, so to hide dirt, Levi dyed it indigo blue.

Rivets. Miners and other laborers wanted heavy-duty pants that would not split where the seams crossed, hence the rivets. Although he took the idea from another tailor, Levi was the first to use the feature in a big way.

After Julius Caesar crossed the Rubicon—and changed the history of the western world forever—he toasted his officers. With beer!

Was it lager or ale?

Beer: A Human Bond?

Caesar was not the only beer aficionado. Queen Elizabeth I, when she traveled, would send staff on ahead to test which local beers were up to snuff. Finland's national epic, the "Kavela," devotes 200 verses to the origin of the world, and 400 to the origin of beer. Harvard had its own brew house in 1674 (and five beer halls, all burned by rioting divinity students!) The first beer brewed in America was in Virginia in 1587. That same year the colonists sent a request back to England for better stuff. Although Belgians make the most kinds of ale and lager (400+), the Czechs drink the most per capita. They drink it mostly in pubs, a fact that has special interest in the Canadian province of Manitoba where, in 2005, it was still illegal to drink beer in an outdoor privy.

Had to be ale. Ale is top-fermented because the yeast rises. With lager it's the opposite; the yeast settles to the bottom. For centuries, brewers made ale only, because all yeasts rose during fermentation. No one understood why that happened but since English brewers called ale *godisgood*, it's clear they weren't about to look a gift horse in the mouth. The first recorded mention of lager is from the thirteenth century in Bavaria, where beer-makers began to store or "lager" their brew in cool, mountain caves. In this environment the yeast settled, producing a clearer liquid and a different, usually sharper taste. Not until artificial refrigeration came along in the nineteenth century did lager brewing become widespread, with the U.S. dominating production, a fact which may explain why American beer has a reputation for lagers so bland they must be served ice-cold. Other countries lean more to ales and tangier lagers, both of which lose taste if over-refrigerated.

Unless you are the one in five hundred who is allergic to aspirin, it's likely you have taken it at one time or another, and it's also likely your great-grandparents did, too, for acetylsalicylic acid was developed over a century and a half ago.

Where?

Recommended by the American Medical Association?

When importation of the cough syrup into America was banned in 1924, regular customers turned to Coca-Cola® for their buzz, only to discover that this product had undergone major change. John Styth Pemberton, who first brewed up the concoction in his backyard (registered in 1885 as "French Wine Coca"), had included both cocaine and caffeine, thereby justifying his claim for it as an "Ideal Nerve and Tonic Stimulant," but the cocaine was long gone by 1924.

Was Aspirin a War Casualty?

Bayer had twenty years of success with aspirin, but lost the trademark in 1919 as part of Germany's reparation payments following World War I (a sore point that Hitler used to advantage later on). International drug companies then held a war of their own until a court decision ruled that Aspirin is aspirin and nobody owns the name. Throughout all the fuss, Bayer survived quite comfortably selling a popular cough syrup, a principal ingredient of which was heroin.

France. In 1853, chemist Charles Gerhardt synthesized acetylsalicylic acid in his lab at the University of Montpelier. He got a publication out of it, but didn't think much of the discovery, and since the rest of the world didn't either, he shelved it. Forty years later, a chemist named Felix Hoffman working at Bayer in Germany was desperate to relieve his father's agony from arthritis and happened to read Gerhardt's article.

Brothers Gaston and Louis Chevrolet had no trouble picking a name for the cars they were making early in the twentieth century, nor did the Dodge brothers, Horace and John. Their names are still on cars today. That's not the case for brothers Fred and August Duesenberg, whose wickedly fast luxury autos hit the market in 1919, or for brothers Freelan and Francis.

What did Freelan and Francis call the cars they made?

What is it about brothers?

America's first gasoline-powered car was developed, not in Detroit but in Springfield, MA, by brothers Charles and Frank Duryea. They called it the "Duryea." On the other hand, Englishman David Salomons (who invented the light socket switch) made the world's first electric car in 1874, a one-horsepower, three-wheeler, and didn't call it anything. He must have been an only child.

What the world needs now . . . ?

The Stanley had no transmission, no spark plugs, no gearshift, and only fifteen moving parts. It generated no pollution, no noise, and real power. For anyone nuts enough to try it on the roads of the day, a Stanley could hit 130 mph on the straightaway without breaking a sweat. And it had a lifetime guarantee; if anything went wrong with a Stanley, the brothers would fix it for free. The downside for this car was the time it took to get the steam up and the need to water up frequently. Negative advertising by gasoline-fuel manufacturers in Detroit made much of this, along with feeding a suspicion that steamers blew up. Ironically, these shortcomings had been corrected by the time the last Stanley rolled off the line in 1925, after Francis and Freelan finally surrendered the field to the gas guys. What made this outcome inevitable was that the eccentric Stanley brothers really didn't care about winning. Even in the final, losing years they would only sell a steamer to a customer if they felt like it.

The Stanley Steamer.

Their first model rolled out of the shop in 1897. Not a new idea—that happened in France over a century before—but the Stanley brothers produced an American car that would have great credibility today.

A chemical engineer says "tetrafluoroethylene." *The Guinness Book of World Records* dubs it "the slipperiest substance on earth." The rest of us call it Teflon®.

If nothing sticks to Teflon, then how does Teflon stick to a frying pan?

Did Pyrex® Keep Teflon in the Dark?

Around the same time Teflon was discovered—and ignored—the science weenies at Corning in New York were working like fury to improve on a kind of glass cookware that they were convinced was revolutionary. By the time Pyrex was introduced to the world in 1936, they had boiled and fried more than nine tons of potatoes to be sure they had gotten it right.

Where Was Teflon Discovered?

In 1938, what would one day be known as Teflon was discovered by accident at the Du Pont company in New Jersey, but the lab was working on coolant gases for refrigerators at the time, so the strange new substance was shelved. The product ended up in the hands of a French manufacturer of pots and pans, but the company's president, an avid fisherman, only used it to coat fish hooks to keep them from tangling. He took his wife fishing one day and it was she who thought of putting Teflon on frying pans. Today the substance is used in everything from space suits, human hearts and light bulbs, to the fifteen thousand joints in the Statue of Liberty.

Molecular behavior. It's complicated, so if high school chemistry put you to sleep, then skip this paragraph. In simple terms (although "simple" doesn't exist in chemistry) Teflon contains non-stick molecules which, in defiance of their description, stick to other non-stick molecules. So by first putting a layer of primer with non-stick molecules on the inside bottom of the frying pan and then the Teflon on top, the non-stick molecules that make up Teflon bind to their relatives in the primer. But food molecules do not stick to non-stick molecules, so the result is a happy chemical world: the Teflon sticks to the primer; the food does not stick to the Teflon. (Yawns permissible here.)

8

Historians generally agree that Karl Benz built the world's first motorcar.

Who built the first motorcycle?

Should Bikers be Avoided?

Motorcycle gangs developed first in California with a rag-tag bunch initially known as the "Pissed-Off Bastards of Bloomington," later evolving into the Hell's Angels. Whether all bike riders should be avoided or not is moot, but an incident in North Africa during World War II may be instructive. An Australian infantryman was spotted by German troops tearing down a desert road on a Daimler he'd co-opted from the enemy. A German officer shouted at him to stop, first in German, then in Italian, to which the Australian responded—in English—"Piss off, mate!" Whether it was the words, the tone, or the Daimler, the officer did just that, confirming that with motorbikes, style is everything.

Motorbike Mania?

Daimler's bike was started with a running push, a somewhat unsophisticated method, but considerably safer than that used by competing models that appeared soon after Daimler's. To start these contraptions the gas line had to be heated with an open flame. Risk, however, did not deter early motorcycle enthusiasts: first commercial production, Munich, 1894; first distance race, Paris to Nantes and back, 1896; first fatality, Exeter, England, 1899; first military use of motorcycles, the Boer War in 1900. Just a hundred years later, motorcycles were everywhere (annual sales of new bikes in the U.S. broke the one-million mark in 2003).

Gottlieb Daimler. Benz drove his car on the streets of Munich, Germany, in 1886. Daimler's son, Paul, took the motorcycle for a spin the year before, thereby becoming not just the first person to drive one, but the first kid to ask Dad for the keys.

9

To most people, IOC stands for the International Olympic Committee. To others, IOC stands for the International Ornithological Congress, and to a group of environmentalists concerned about global warming, IOC means the International Ozone Commission. Not to be outdone, there's the IOOC.

What's the IOOC?

And What of other Virgins?

Although science has yet to demonstrate a similar longevity factor in other forms of nature, it has established that female mice which remain *hymen intacta* do in fact live longer. Comparative data for humans is very scant, although certain known cases provide food for thought. Sir Isaac Newton, for example, a life-long virgin (by his own account) lived to be 85 at a time when life expectancy was half that. Victorian poet Alfred Tennyson remained a virgin until age 41 when he married Emily Selwood. He then lived another 42 years.

Has *virgin* olive oil never been . . . well, touched?

The virginity rating of olive oil refers to its percentage of acid, with virgin under 2% and extra virgin at .8% or below. Perhaps more interesting to the study of virginity in a broader sense, virgin olive oils consistently outlive other grades before turning rancid.

The International Olive Oil Council, which monitors production, helps establish prices and ensures that the quality of olive oil is maintained across the world.

Quite logically, the IOOC is headquartered in Spain because that's where almost half the world's olives are grown (unlike OPEC, which usually meets in Austria, a country that has never ever produced a drop of oil of any kind). Still, the olive oil business has curiosities of its own, one of which is that most of the olive oil bottles in North American supermarkets say "imported from Italy" on the label. But what that means is that the oil inside was bottled in Italy, the number-two grower, and more than likely comes from Spain or possibly from the number-three producer, Greece.

CATEGORY 10

Legends

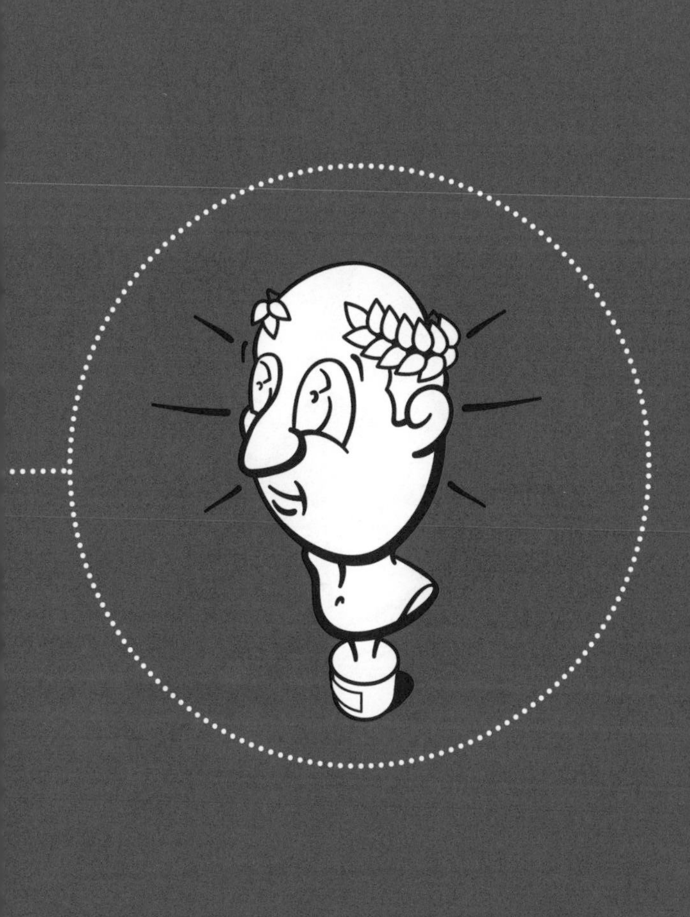

1

Legend has it that Saint George was the knight in shining armor that killed a fire-breathing dragon and saved a damsel in distress.

Who was the damsel?

An Extremely Busy Patron Saint?

Few saints have more expected of them than Saint George, who is the patron of England, Portugal, Germany, Genoa, Venice, and Aragon as well as of soldiers, farmers, and boy scouts. Saint Dunstan, on the other hand, is patron saint of blacksmiths and lighthouse keepers, and therefore, should you be looking to choose a patron saint, Dunstan would conceivably have more time.

Did George exist?

Most scholars agree there was a George, that he was a Christian, and that he was put to death for this commitment in Palestine early in the third century. The dragon story came along a millennium or so later in a book of legends. Although the story has many variations, the basic one tells that George wandered into the city of Sylene, in the Roman province of Lybia, just as a local dragon had upped his demands from two sheep a day to human beings. An obvious choice for any dragon with a subliminal death wish would be the king's daughter, which is how Sabra came to be carried off. Into the breach leapt—or rather, rode—George, who elected to combine rescue with opportunity, for instead of killing the dragon he merely wounded it. Then he took off Sabra's belt (this is not the opportunity referred to above) and used it to drag the unfortunate monster back to Sylene where, after extracting a promise from the king and his citizens to become Christians, he finished it off. George then married Sabra, and the dragon's carcass was carried off in four carts. (Why four? It's a legend.)

Sabra. The dragon, understandably, was a no-name. Still, his (or her) surviving relatives must have heaved a fiery sigh of relief when the Vatican lowered George's high profile in its calendar of saints after centuries of celebration. Not that dragons are out of the woods, for the Church of England still keeps George front and center.

2

Jackie Robinson won Rookie of the Year in the same year he is credited with breaking the color barrier in big league baseball. That was in 1947. The following year, the rookie crown was offered to another African-American, but he turned it down.

Who was that?

So who's on first—really?

Recognizing the Negro Leagues would stir up a statistical hornet's nest for baseball. For one thing, it would have to consider disqualifying Jackie Robinson's rookie award retroactively, because he played pro ball in 1945 for the KC Monarchs. But then, he really wasn't first in any case. That claim actually belongs to Moses Fleetwood Walker, who caught (barehanded) for the Toledo Blue Stockings in 1884, a pro team in a pro league. Walker was a college-educated man who played in four different leagues before being barred for his color in 1890.

Should the Negro League Be Acknowledged?

Major league baseball still has not resolved the matter of incorporating statistics from the former Negro Leagues, despite the achievements of some astonishing players like Satchel Paige, or Dick "Cannonball" Redding who had 30 career no-hitters and once struck out 25 batters in a single game. Or pitcher Wilbur Rogan, who had a career 113-45 won/lost record with the Kansas City Monarchs and never batted under .300! Still another eyebrow raiser: of the documented exhibition games between Negro League and "regular" major league teams, the former won over 60 per cent of the time.

"Satchel" Paige.

Leroy "Satchel" Paige was 42 years old in 1948, and had already acquired simply awesome stats in the Negro Leagues. He didn't really feel he was a rookie. "[I] didn't know who those gentlemen had in mind," was his classy explanation of why he said no. Paige began his pro career as a pitcher with the Birmingham Black Barons in 1926 (part of his training regimen was throwing strikes over a bottle cap), and retired in 1965 at age 59, pitching for the Kansas City Athletics.

3

Asked for the biggest name in psychoanalysis, odds are about 99 to1 you will opt for its founder, Sigmund Freud.

If he was *first*, in what branch of medicine did he get his start?

"Lie down there and we'll talk."

Hollywood did much to paint a picture of psychiatric treatment as one where patients lie on a couch in a darkened room while they unburden their souls. Sigmund Freud is credited with originating the technique, and it enjoys extensive justifying literature in journals of psychiatry. Yet Freud himself said the reason he placed his patients that way was because he couldn't stand looking at human faces for eight hours a day.

American women are scary?

Fame brought Freud across the Atlantic in 1909 to lecture, a visit which provided opportunity for some unsolicited analysis in which he deemed the U.S.A. a "gigantic mistake." It could be he formed that opinion because of a prostate condition he suffered at the time, for he complained constantly that American cities did not have enough urinals. What bothered him far more was the way American women were allowed to treat men. Although he was impressed by what he thought was their more positive attitude to sex, observing that they "haven't got the European woman's constant fear of seduction," at the same time they "lead men around by the nose [which is why] marriage is so unsuccessful in America." Such feminist freedom must have caused Freud problems of his own, for during the visit he confessed to Carl Jung that he was troubled with dreams about prostitutes. (When Jung suggested "doing something about it," Freud was horrified, replying that for a married man such a response was out of the question.)

Neurology. Early in his career in Vienna, Freud began urging his patients to dig into their past, especially into their dreams. One result was the famous *Interpretation of Dreams*. It was published in 1900, but is still mandatory reading today (not by Nazis though; Hitler banned it, along with the entire field of psychoanalysis, in 1933).

4

The great hero of Switzerland earned that status centuries ago by obeying the command of a cruel governor and shooting an apple off his son's head with his crossbow. (He then shot the governor.) The hero's name is William Tell. The son had to be just as heroic.

What was his name?

Should We Tell the Swiss?

Given the experience of Uriel Freudenberger, it is probably a bad idea to argue about the William Tell legend in Switzerland. In 1760, in the Swiss canton of Uri, Freudenberger was sentenced to be burned at the stake for publishing his opinion that the story is actually Danish. (In fact, the legend appears in Norse, Finnish, British, and Russian folklore, among others.)

How did Detroit Get into It?

Italian composer Gioacchino Rossini gave the legend a giant musical boost in 1829 with his opera about William Tell. It's rarely performed, even in Switzerland, but everybody knows the overture, thanks to radio station WXYZ in Detroit, which first used it in 1933 as introductory theme music for the "Lone Ranger" western series. The radio show (and later, the television series) created such a powerful link with the "Overture to William Tell" that as late as the 1980s, in an informal survey of freshmen music students at the University of Toronto, over two-thirds identified the overture as "the Lone Ranger music."

Walter. To be fair, you should get points if you said "no name at all" for despite fierce (as in really fierce) insistence by the Swiss, especially at the department of tourism, there's no real evidence that William—or Walter for that matter—ever existed. Notwithstanding the alleged Tell artifacts in museums and the many Tell festivals and other celebrations, the legend is just that, a legend. A chronicle of 1482 was first to mention the story, placing the event in the year 1296. The classic form of the legend appeared in 1735 and gives the date as 1307. However it was an 1804 play by Friederich Schiller that gave the tale international popularity. Schiller's play was also the first version of the story to put a name on the son: hence, Walter.

5

William H. Bonney was "Billy the Kid." The "kid" part is easy to understand because he was indeed, just a kid. John Henry "Doc" Halliday was a dentist, so the "Doc" nickname makes sense, too. Yet another legendary gunman in the old west was William Barclay Masterson, far better known as "Bat."

Why was he known as "Bat?"

Passing into Legend?

Eighteen months after the J.T. Grant episode, and after allegedly killing twenty-one men, Billy was himself dispatched by Sheriff Pat Garrett. "Bat" Masterson, on the other hand, after allegedly killing over thirty (only two authenticated), moved to New York City where he became a sports writer. He died of a heart attack, cane in hand, in 1921.

Were the lights on?

There is evidence that the wannabes taking on the likes of Masterson were not too bright, either before or after cranial persuasion with a cane. Among the more impressive examples is J.T. Grant, who challenged Billy the Kid in a saloon at Fort Sumner, NM on January 24, 1880. Billy accepted on condition he could first have a look at Grant's gun. During the examination the cylinder was surreptitiously adjusted so the hammer would strike an empty chamber on the next shot.

Billy won.

From the cane he carried.

The cane was not just an ornament. He needed it to get around. On a January night in 1876, in Sweetwater, Texas, Masterson was escorting a working girl named Molly Brennan when the two ran afoul of U.S. Cavalry sergeant Melvin King, a man with a drinking problem and what appears to be a need for anger management therapy. During their argument, King started firing, accidentally killing Molly with one shot and smashing Masterson's hip with another. "Bat" put King away with a single shot, but the hip wound made him limp noticeably for the rest of his life. The cane, as it turned out, became a useful supplement to the flashy pair of nickel-plated Colt Peacemakers he carried during his career as a lawman. He was able to intimidate more potential lawbreakers with the cane than with his guns.

6

No legend is more thoroughly entrenched than the one that covers the origin of the lowly sandwich. John Montagu (1718-92) the Fourth Earl of Sandwich, was feeling peckish one night in 1762, but couldn't tear himself away from the craps table, so one of his servants came up with the idea of putting some meat between two slices of bread. That supposedly gave him sustenance, and at the same time left one hand free to toss the dice.

What kind of sandwich was it?

More on the Sandwich?

Peanut butter was a big hit at the World's Fair in 1904, but the first mention of peanut butter and jelly sandwiches in American media didn't appear until 1940. A lot has changed since, for nutritionists estimate that the average kid today eats over 1500 pb&js before finishing high school.

More on the Earl?

His Lordship was a known gambler, but had an even wider reputation for corruption, mismanagement, bribery, and other niceties. Among his notable activities was being First Lord of the Admiralty during the American Revolution, and we all know how that turned out. To lovers of the great quip, however, the Fourth of Earl of Sandwich has become an icon for setting himself up with one of the best straight lines in history. While quarreling with John Wilkes, Lord Mayor of London, he said, "You, Wilkes, will either die on the gallows or from syphilis." To which the mayor replied, "That depends, Your Lordship, on whether I embrace your principles or your mistress."

Roast beef.

That's the legend, anyway, but there's no hard proof. It could have been mutton, too, or cheese, for both were common snacks of the day. For sure it wasn't peanut butter, because that didn't come along until the 1904 World's Fair in St. Louis. Also of note is that although the word sandwich is often traced to the earl, the idea is not, for the Romans had a similar snack two thousand years before. It was called an offula, which may be why the word didn't catch on. (They had ketchup too, called liquamen, but that word was never picked up, either.)

7

Orson Welles was already on the high profile highway when he terrified the whole of northeastern U.S.A. on Sunday, October 30, 1938, with a radio program about an invasion from Mars. The program was "Mercury Theater of the Air," which broadcast every Sunday night at 8 p.m. on CBS. At the time Mercury Theater was having a serious ratings problem, because at 8 p.m. on Sunday nights, most of America was tuned in to NBC.

What was this popular show on NBC?

Is it easier to believe than think?

An elaborate hoax published by the *New York Sun* in August, 1835, told readers that life had been discovered on the moon (including winged humans and two-legged beavers). When the hoax was exposed after a run of several weeks, it was also revealed that the most convinced and enthusiastic believers by far had been the faculty and students of Yale University.

Did Opportunity Knock?

Welles knew that dial spinners listening to "The Chase and Sanborn Hour" always got fidgety at 8:12 p.m. because that's when Bergen broke for a guest, usually a singer. It was precisely at 8:12 that Professor Pierson, who was live on scene, saw creatures crawl out of the cylinders. The rest, as they say, could only happen in America. Of the estimated ten million listeners who switched to—then stayed—with CBS (obviously, the show worked) over a million hit the streets, hid in their basements, or took shelter in churches and police stations—despite four specific caveats during the Mercury Theater show: "This is purely a fictional play."

"The Chase and Sanborn Hour," starring Edgar Bergen and Charlie McCarthy.

Bergen with his puppets, the wisecracking Charlie, and the terminally stupid Mortimer Snerd, practically owned the airwaves on Sunday nights, and although Welles always denied it, his "invasion" over on CBS seemed remarkably well timed to penetrate the competition. Mercury Theater opened that night, as many radio shows did, with a live orchestra (Ramon Raquello from the Park Plaza in New York). But the music was regularly interrupted by bulletins about strange eruptions on Mars, interspersed by interviews with a "Professor Pierson" who was keeping an eye on some strange, humming cylinders that had fallen from the skies into New Jersey.

8

No list of legendary figures is complete without Julius Caesar. Charlemagne is an easy pick too, and so is King David. And, of course, Alexander the Great.

Where, in Las Vegas, would you find these four legends *together*?

Photo-op?

Interestingly, although England has had six Georges on the throne, not one was ever given a label that stuck. George III, however, can lay claim to an alternative marker of some distinction, because during the American Revolution, his image appeared on the bottom of chamber pots. They were a big seller.

How do Kings get Labeled?

Charlemagne and Alexander have been dubbed "great," while neither David nor Julius Caesar has ever acquired a descriptive title. This could be because they are so famous, a label is unnecessary. That's not the case for lesser types. The many Charles's and Louis's of Europe for example, have included a Bold, a Wise, a Fair, a Noble, a Pious, a Strict, and a Well-Beloved. Not to ignore the other side of the coin, the Charles's and Louis's also have a Sluggard, a Simple, a Fat, and a Quarreler. Charlemagne's father was Pepin the Short (he was shorter than his sword), and his mother was Bertha of the Big Foot. Ruling families, it seems, were keen on repeating names in order to honor their predecessors. A less flattering theory is that they were too inbred to come up with any new ones. Whichever view is accurate, the fact is the common people, because there were so many rulers with the same name, had to come up with descriptive titles as a kind of scorecard to help them understand who was doing what, when, and to whom. Thus when Germany's Charles the Bald got into a war with Spain's Wilfrid the Hairy in the year 878, everybody knew what—and who—was what.

In a deck of playing cards. Charlemagne is the model for the king of hearts, and David for the king of spades. Alexander is the king of clubs, and Caesar, the king of diamonds. The tradition is centuries old.

9

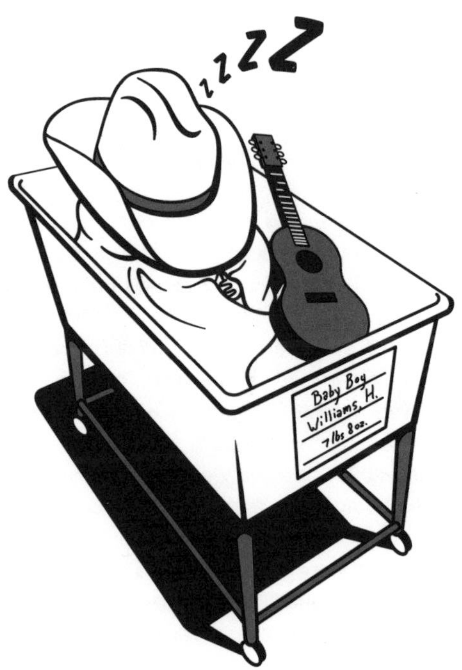

Hank Williams is not just a legend in country music, he is *the* legend. The "Williams" is accurate; he was the son of Lon and Lillie Williams. But "Hank" is a diminutive of his first name.

What is Hank's real first name?

Ridin', Drinkin', Shootin'

Hank was born with mild *spina bifida*, a condition aggravated by a horseback-riding injury. Doctors treated the resulting pain with mega-doses of drugs, a therapy that Hank enhanced with booze. The combination may or may not have been the immediate cause of his penchant for shooting, but it certainly didn't stop it, either. He had a particularly annoying habit (to the hospitality industry) of peppering hotel rooms. On one occasion he fired at a maid who wisely clobbered him with a lamp before he could take a second shot. Rehab never seemed to help. Contributing to his legend was the attempt at Vanderbilt Hospital, where he checked out while the admission papers were being completed and went on a three-week bender.

Hank Williams Junior (b. 1949) is officially Randall Hank Williams and Hank Williams III (b. 1972) is Shelton Hank Williams. Both their birth certificates are spelled correctly.

A Legend for all the Right/Wrong Reasons?

That Hank Williams was in a class all his own, both as a songwriter and a performer, there is no doubt, but he is just as legendary, maybe even more so, for his lifestyle. According to the late Minnie Pearl, "He just destroyed women in the audience." After the show, too, it seems. Although he had married Audrey Mae Sheppard Guy in 1944—in a gas station—his post-performance escapades led to a divorce in 1952. The same year he married Billy Jean Jones Eshmiller (three times on the same day: the two extras were for paying customers in an auditorium in New Orleans.) Right in the middle of all this, one of Hank's interim flames, Bobbie Webb Jett, gave birth to a daughter.

Not Henry. It's Hiram, although his birth certificate in Mount Olive, AL, says "Hiriam" (which the family insisted was a spelling error).

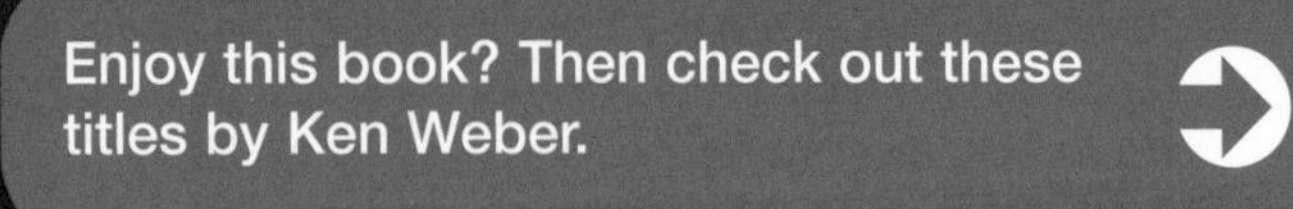
Enjoy this book? Then check out these titles by Ken Weber.

SPORTS
ASTRONAUT SITS DOWN TO GO #1

Five-Minute Mysteries

More Five-Minute Mysteries

Absolutely Amazing Five-Minute Mysteries

Even More Five-Minute Mysteries

Further Five-Minute Mysteries

Utterly Ingenious Five-Minute Mysteries